Mother Was It Worth It?

the sequel to 'Sell the Pig'
and 'Is That Billinge Lump?'

Mother Was It Worth It?

*the sequel to 'Sell the Pig'
and 'Is That Billinge Lump?'*

LIVRES
LEMAS

Tottie Limejuice

Published by LEMAS LIVRES
www.tottielimejuice.com

© Copyright L.M.K. Tither 2014
Cover design DMR Creative

MOTHER WAS IT WORTH IT?
First edition

Cover photo © Tottie Limejuice

ISBN 978-2-901-77314-6

Contents

Dedication

To my mother, Nell Tither. Had it not been for her, I might never have made the decision to move to France. It was her favourite saying which gave rise to the name 'Sell the Pig' for this trilogy of travel memoirs.

'Mother, Mother, it's a bugger, sell the pig and buy me out.'

Nell Tither 1917 - 2011

About the Author

Tottie Limejuice is the pen-name of Lesley Tither, a former journalist turned freelance copywriter and copy editor, who lives in the Auvergne region of central France. Passionate about wildlife and the countryside, she enjoys walks and camping with her dogs, and organic gardening.

'Mother, was it worth it?' is the third book in the Sell the Pig series which began with 'Sell the Pig' and continued with 'Is That Billinge Lump?'

If you have enjoyed reading it, please consider leaving a review on Amazon.

Tottie Limejuice is also the author of 'Press Releases: An Idiot's Guide - Free Publicity Through the Media'

If you would like to get in touch, you can do so by:

Email – tottielimejuice@gmail.com

Website - http://tottielimejuice.com/

Facebook - https://www.facebook.com/tottie.limejuice

Chapter One
Night, night, Ducky

Nine o'clock in the morning and no sign of my brother. Not of itself unusual; his out of control drinking meant I often didn't see him emerge from his flat for days at a time.

But today was different. Today was our mother's funeral, and I needed him to be up, washed, dressed and presentable, or 'tidy', as they say in south Wales, where my brother had lived for the past thirty or so years.

Four years ago, almost to the day, my brother and I had made the momentous – some might say insane – decision to move our elderly mother from the UK to start a new life in France. We'd been appalled by the level of care available to her in the over-stretched, under-resourced hospitals and care homes in England and Wales. So we'd found a new family home in central France's Auvergne, which we called the Pink House, where she had enjoyed four years of a vastly improved quality of life. I had been her full-time carer, assisted by some excellent auxiliary home carers and a wonderful doctor, who regularly made house calls, even for non-emergencies.

Despite her vascular dementia, which gave her a fascination for 'rude words' like 'bum' and 'bugger', and the behaviour of a naughty child showing off, Mother had thrived in France, although most of the time she had no idea she was living abroad. She would sit in the sunshine on the warm, sheltered patio of the Pink House, gazing out at the chain of volcanoes and frequently asking: 'Is that Billinge Lump?', referring to a famous landmark in her home town of St Helens in Lancashire.

But as she approached her ninety-fourth birthday, her health had started to decline, she'd started refusing all medication and had slipped quietly away, in her own bed, just four days after her birthday.

She'd died at four o'clock in the morning and as she was finally at rest, I'd left her quietly until her morning carer, the formidable Mme LaC, had arrived shortly after eight, for her usual morning duties of getting her up, washed and dressed. I knew Mme LaC would know the correct procedure to follow, and she did indeed.

Mme LaC was large of both stature and personality, and breezed through our lives with a dynamic energy which seemed at odds with her size. Within minutes, she had telephoned a doctor for the required death certificate, and an undertaker to come and take Mother away to the chapel of rest. In between, she had made a few adjustments to Mother's seemingly peacefully sleeping form which, she explained to me, in possibly slightly more detail than I really needed, was to make the undertaker's task more simple and less forceful.

My brother lived in a small apartment on the ground floor of the Pink House. I'd seen him earlier that morning, when I took my dog, Ci, out for his morning walk, and told him that Mother had gone to Billinge Lump. My views on death and the afterlife are a bit woolly so I'd decided it would be nice to think that Mother had gone to a place which had been so important in her childhood and which she had shared with my brother and me when we were small. We had many family memories of going to pick blackberries on Billinge Lump with Mother, Father, Granny and our Auntie Ethel.

The still form now lying in the motorised hospital bed in my mother's room was so unlike my energetic, funny, lively mother that I preferred a mental image of her doing something she had always loved. And, most importantly for her, being finally reunited with her own mother, the person she'd talked about incessantly as her mind wandered further away from recent reality.

In France, a funeral has to take place within a week of death. I'd expected some sort of a vacuum immediately following Mother's death, as my waking and many of my sleeping hours had been taken up with caring for her during the past four years. Instead, there was quite a whirlwind of activity, starting with a visit the same morning to the funeral director's to make all the arrangements. We decided to have her cremated so that we could, at a future date, return her ashes to her home town for interment in her family grave at the parish church where she had been married.

Our father's ashes were already in the garden of remembrance there. Mother's original wish had been to have her ashes put with those of her late husband, but in later life she seemed to have gone off that idea, and to have rather gone off him, though that might have simply been the dementia at work.

I'd never been to a French funeral and had absolutely no idea of the form. But I did know a lot of Mother's views on such things and knew that she would not want a lot of money spent and would not want it to be too solemn an occasion. Above all, I knew she had a horror of being painted up with make-up, especially bright lipstick, so was at pains to explain this to the funeral director.

My brother and I were both surprised at the speed with which she was prepared for us to see. I had gone through her wardrobe, carefully choosing the clothes she might have picked out herself, at the same time having a wry chuckle to think she would hate her very best clothes to be wasted on a cremation. All of her other outfits would now be handed on to a deserving charity, as she would have wished.

As she'd become more childlike through dementia, Mother had loved to be surrounded with cuddly toys. In particular, she

3

had a small collection of pigs, which came about because of her favourite saying: 'Mother, Mother, it's a bugger, sell the pig and buy me out!', a telegram home from a young man not enjoying military service, asking his impoverished farming family to pay his release by the only means available to them.

All Mother's French carers now knew this saying and would recite it with her, and would often buy her something pig-related when they spotted it. At the last minute, I tucked one of the little pigs, one which oinked when pressed, into the pocket of her linen jacket. I often wondered what the undertaker made of that.

Mother would have been horrified to know the cost of the coffin which was to contain her for just a few short days. She had died on a Thursday and we were surprised to be given a slot on Monday afternoon for the cremation. In France, the remains of the departed are usually displayed in an open coffin at the chapel of rest for any family or friends who wished to pay their respects.

It wasn't really my thing. In my mind, Mother was now happily picking blackberries on Billinge Lump with her mother and older sister. Of course, it was March, so the blackberries wouldn't be in season, and I kept picturing her wearing a lovely peach-patterned day dress she had made herself, which would not be remotely suitable for autumn on Billinge Lump. But it made a nice, comforting mental image. So for me, the 'person' lying in the chapel, wearing her brown linen jacket, with a little pig hidden in the pocket, with matching slacks, in the least expensive coffin available, which was still horribly ostentatious to her taste, was simply not my mother.

At least the funeral director had listened to what I'd said about make-up. It was minimal, just enough to lift the mortal pallor. They had put a little blue rinse through her hair, something Mother had never liked in her life. But it was at least a steel blue so didn't look too artificial.

We had agreed that the choice of music for the simple

funeral ceremony would be down to my brother, and that I would write a short address, in French, to read out, since it would be all our French friends attending. My brother was the more musically adept of the two of us, although I had attended a very musical school and sung in its choir under the directorship of an acclaimed choral conductor and concert pianist.

The choice of music was going to be tricky since hymns are not international. Our French friends would not know whatever we picked, which meant it would just be me and my brother singing. We could both hold a tune reasonably well, so as long as my brother didn't pick anything too high for my limited contralto range, we thought we would probably be all right.

Neither my brother nor I was particularly religious, although we had been brought up as very high church Church of England. Mother had been a regular church goer until her parish church had swapped its smells and bells ritual of incense and sung Eucharist for happy-clappy family services, with children running riot in the nave and babies wailing so loudly that the older members of the congregation could not hear what was going on.

We settled on 'The Lord's My Shepherd'; to the good old tune of Crimond, and 'Dear Lord and Father of Mankind' to the tune of Repton. My brother was going to make CDs with the hymns on, for the music and a bit of additional lung power. An enthusiastic amateur singer himself, his current role model was Alfie Boe, an English singer, appropriately from Mother's home county of Lancashire. Not a singer with whom I was familiar, and I should have Googled him to check his range, as I later discovered.

As it was all happening in such a whirl, we decided not to have any sort of get-together immediately after the service but instead to postpone it to the following Sunday. We had deliberately not gone out of our way to find other English ex-pats, but amongst those we had met, I counted one couple,

Christine and Geoff, as very dear friends. Christine had been many times to visit Mother and had even stepped into the breach to look after her at very short notice when we were badly let down by her former care service, shortly before she died. Geoff and Christine were away on a very rare holiday on the day of the funeral service, so we decided that by postponing, they would at least be able to attend the tea party.

It had become a tradition to have a tea party every year for Mother's birthday as she loved to be the centre of attention, and adored any excuse to eat cake and receive presents. So the following Sunday we would have a party in honour of her ninety-four years of life, to give her a proper send-off.

So now all that was needed on this, the morning of the funeral, was for my brother to appear, presentably dressed, with the music CDs in his hot little hand. Otherwise I was going to be left struggling valiantly through an *a cappella* solo rendition of both hymns, to the discomfort of the assembled congregation, no doubt.

The splendid Mme LaC had taken it upon herself to drive my brother and me to the crematorium in Clermont-Ferrand. We were also taking with us our eccentric friend, to whom we always referred as Goaty. She kept a few goats in the next but one field to the Pink House and had latched onto us like a leech. She had become something of a nuisance with her frequent visits and demands for attention, but she had always been fond of Mother, and kind to her, so it seemed churlish not to invite her to the funeral.

I wasn't too sure of the dress code for a French funeral, especially in the Auvergne, where dress was always casual. There was no point asking Goaty since her wardrobe varied between outfits revealing rather more bust and thigh than might have been deemed appropriate for someone well into their seventies to shapeless garments smelling strongly of goat and covered in straw. I had opted for an understated pin-striped trouser suit which I hoped would fit the bill.

Mme LaC was punctual, as she always was, and, to my relief, my brother appeared looking very respectable, also in a pin-striped suit, and carrying not only the music CDs but orders of service which he had prepared to hand out to our friends at the ceremony.

We went first to the funeral parlour and, as is the custom, the coffin was still open for us to say our last good-byes to Mother, before it was closed and transferred to the hearse. The coffin was then placed under the raised platform in the back of the hearse so it was not on display as the cortège made its way to its destination.

After we'd exchanged courtesies with the funeral director, my brother drew me aside and said: 'He's been drinking'. And for an alcoholic to be able to smell alcohol on someone else, there has to be a lot of it.

However, there was not much we could do about it at that time so we got into Mme LaC's car once more to follow the hearse to the crematorium. We weren't quite sure if it was the drink or some strange French custom that led the funeral director to drive all the way round the first roundabout when he should have taken the first exit, but we did manage the journey without incident and arrived safely to find friends waiting.

Several of the young carers who had looked after Mother during her time in France were there to pay their respects, as were the ladies from the English conversation group which I had been running. That group consisted of several retired ladies in their fifties and sixties as well as two delightful teenage sisters. As it was a school day, the girls were not able to be present but their mother had very kindly come along to represent them.

The French had certainly never seen a send-off such as we gave to Mother. I wanted it to be in keeping with her lighter side, not too sad and solemn. We asked Goaty to say a few words first, which she did. Then I gave my little address, in French.

Mother had always been in denial about her age, and even once she turned ninety she could have passed for much younger. So when I told her, on her last birthday, that she was ninety-four, she came out with one of her characteristic sayings, as I reminded our assembled friends: 'Ninety-four my bum!', and when I asked her how old she was really, she said immediately: 'Twenty-one!'

She'd missed out on a final birthday party, as by then she was too frail to get out of bed. So I asked everyone to sing 'Happy Birthday' to her, one final time. Then my brother and I sang Crimond, without too many problems, as the range was doable for both of us.

Then Alfie Boe started up with 'Dear Lord and Father' and my heart sank. With his high tenor range, I was going to have to strain vocal chords to the maximum to get the higher notes to match him, especially as when we reached the top notes of the fifth line, my brother mumbled: 'I can't do this' and stopped singing. There were five verses in all, which I was now having to screech my way through on my own, with each subsequent top note getting harder for me to attain.

As the final verse approached, with its climatic build-up to:

'let sense be dumb, let flesh retire;
speak through the earthquake, wind, and fire,
O still, small voice of calm,'

I gave my brother a prod of encouragement and a muttered 'go for it' to get him to join in at the end.

Then the service was over and our funeral director was inviting us all, one at a time, to approach the coffin and say a last few words, starting with the family.

My brother went first, leaving me to ponder on what words would be fitting. We'd never been a particularly close or affectionate family; I could never recall a single occasion when my mother had told me she loved me. She probably did, it was just not her way to say so, so I never recall having said it to her. In her later years, she had become very difficult and resentful towards me as she felt increasingly frustrated at her helplessness, so we had not had an easy time.

At some point in her life Mother must have encountered someone from the East Midlands, where a friendly greeting is often: 'Ey up, mi duck', and had picked up the use of the word 'ducky' as an affectionate term.

So when it was my turn to approach, I simply laid a hand on the coffin and said what I had said to her every night for the past four years, as I'd checked that she was settled down for the night, surrounded by her cuddly toys and squeaky pigs.

'Night night, ducky.'

Chapter Two
St Loo and St Dongle

Four o'clock in the morning and I was catapulted from the comatose sleep of the exhausted into a semi-awake somnambulism which took me through the door into the next bedroom before I realised that my mother was no longer there.

I had stripped the bed after she had been taken away so there was nothing but an empty hospital bed. It was one which could be adjusted electrically for height and angle, with detachable cot sides to prevent her from falling out when her nights were very disturbed by her dementia. She was sometimes keen to get up to go to work at Cambridge Road post office, where she had not worked since the 1930s.

Four o'clock was the time at which I had found her dead, shortly after I had gone next door to my room for some essential sleep. It was to become my witching hour for many months, the time at which something deep in my subconscious would snap me awake from the deepest of sleep, even one induced by the mild sleeping pills I tried in order to break the cycle.

Mother's collection of cuddly toys was lined up on the bed – Baby, the big collie dog, Big Teddy, Blue Teddy, the little girly teddy in a pink house coat who somehow had never had a name, Tinker, the German Shepherd puppy, and her two remaining pink pigs. I wondered if they missed her.

But she was gone and there were changes afoot and

decisions to be made. Caring for Mother had been my full-time occupation for four years, apart from some of the copywriting I did whenever I could fit it in, to give myself some sort of income so I could pay into the expensive French system for healthcare and social security benefits. With Mother gone, I was effectively redundant as a carer.

The original plan had been for me to run either B&B or apartment hire using the empty top floor suite of the Pink House, to get some income from the property. After several drunken threats by my brother to throw me out of the house, despite me being mother's full-time carer, effectively making me homeless, I had taken the plunge and bought myself a property of my own.

Tottie's Grottage, as it was affectionately known amongst my friends, was on the eastern edge of the Livradois-Forez Regional Nature Park in the Auvergne, some fifty miles from the Pink House. It was going to be wonderful, with its idyllic views west to the sun setting over the volcanic chain.

There were a couple of minor matters which would stop me moving into it immediately. Well, fairly major matters, actually. Three in particular. The grottage (short for grotty cottage), although sporting a very smart new roof and tasteful pale pink new rendering, had no electricity, no water and no sanitation of any description. Needless to say, there was no telephone either. So, much as I love camping out and roughing it, it was not going to be practical in its present state as I relied entirely on internet access to carry out my work.

I was also concerned about how my brother was going to cope on his own. He had made no friends, not having the social skills to do so, and had always been very close to Mother. I was not sure if her loss would plunge him further into a drink-fuelled depression or whether it might finally force him into making a decision to take control of his life and get it back on track.

But first we needed to host a tea party for our friends to

give Mother a final send-off, and then my brother would return to the UK with her ashes to have them interred in the family grave with her mother, father, older sister and one of her brothers.

It was a warm and pleasant day for the tea party so we were able to sit outside on the patio. Mother would have loved it! Her favourite carers came, as did my English students, and this time the girls were able to come too, with their mother, as it was a Sunday. My English friends Christine and Geoff came, and Goaty, of course, once more showing a bit of thigh and a lot of bosom.

My brother and I, both enthusiastic pastry cooks, he formally professionally, me an experienced amateur, baked no end of cakes, or as an old Derbyshire lady I used to know would have said, 'galores' of cakes. Everyone brought gifts. The girls had selected a beautiful rose for my garden, called *Sourire d'Orchidée*, orchid's smile. *Sourire* is one of those French words which catches out the unwary as it is so similar to *souris*, a mouse. Many a French learner has earned a quizzical glance for dithering over whether they were about to say a funny remark had made them mouse or made them smile.

One of my brother's cakes looked particularly delicious. It was made with mandarin oranges and was a rich, dark colour which reminded me of the ginger cake our Luxembourg granny used to make. That had become a bit of a family joke. When our parents were courting, Granny used to make her special ginger cake whenever Mother visited, and always served it warm from the oven. Unfortunately, Mother didn't like it, but was too polite to say so, so just kept toying with it for as long as she could, when Granny would say it was not as good cold.

'Have a piece of your favourite ginger cake, it's no good when it's cold,' became one of our family sayings.

My brother couldn't account at all for the colour of his cake as he had no recollection of including any ingredient which would have turned the mixture so dark. Should he serve it to our guests and risk giving them food poisoning, or worse? In the end he took the risk and served it. It was pronounced delicious and devoured down to the very last crumb. All of the tea party guests are still alive!

And once the guests had gone, and my brother had carefully loaded Mother's ashes, in their biodegradable urn, into his motorhome, The Dingley, I was alone in the Pink House for the first time in four years, apart from the cats and my dog Ci, with no ties to bind me and no routine to follow.

I was a bit worried about that biodegradable urn. We chose it because we thought it would appeal to Mother, being the least expensive, and also because it would allow her, literally, to return to her roots in Eccleston, St Helens. But my brother is not the fastest driver in the world, and goes to great lengths to avoid motorway travel. Most visitors make the journey from Calais to the Pink House in about seven hours, using the excellent *autoroute* network. My brother has been known to take three days. I just hoped the undertaker was right in telling us the urn did not start to biodegrade until it was placed in the ground. I didn't like to think of Mother making her final journey slowly trickling out of the urn into a Tesco's carrier bag.

My brother had decided to make a last sentimental drive to Billinge Lump, with Mother's ashes still on board, before taking them to the churchyard to be laid to rest. We somehow felt that if there was still some tenuous connection to the present world and wherever Mother was now, she would appreciate the gesture.

With my time my own, I could also start taking possession, of sorts, of Tottie's Grottage. I was eager to begin the long process of bringing it up to a basic standard where I could live in it, rather than just going there and camping out, as I had been doing since I had bought it, just three months earlier.

One of the first things I wanted to do was to secure the medium sized plot of land in front of the grottage, which I hoped would one day be a garden but was at present nothing more than grass and cow parsley. It overlooked an adjoining field, which had strands of barbed wire to contain occasional cattle, but I wanted to be able to let my dog Ci run loose in the garden as much as possible. So because he liked to chase cars, bicycles and particularly joggers, it would have to be made secure.

In keeping with my future rustic home, I wanted things to be old-style, certainly not modern. I'd discovered the wonderful French online selling site *Le Bon Coin*, which was actually where I'd first seen the advert for the grottage, and found on there an old set of wrought iron gates which I bought as they would look just the part. There weren't any gateposts yet. In fact there was very little of anything. But a pair of gates was a start. I just had to find a way to get them to my property, as they were too large to fit into my Opel Combo van, and far too heavy for me to manoeuvre on my own.

It seemed Mme LaC's talents were not confined to looking after my mother, helping to organise her funeral, and generally taking care of me through the brief time she had been a part of our lives. She, or rather her husband, was also the proud owner of a Peugeot Expert van, which could accommodate the gates. For little more than the cost of the diesel, she would happily help me to take the gates over to the grottage, together with some other essential bits and pieces, like a bed.

Whilst living in Market Rasen, Lincolnshire, I had bought myself two antique pine beds, probably Dutch in origin, with high sides and tall, carved headboards. They would fit in perfectly with the character of the grottage. One, which was slightly larger than the other, was what I slept in at the Pink House so would stay there for the time being. The slightly smaller one, a spare guest bed, came over on the trip with the gates so I would, at least, have a bed to sleep in.

If Mme LaC had thought me, thus far, slightly eccentric but relatively sane, leading her in convoy through the twisty turny roads of the Livradois-Forez and arriving at my little grottage in the middle of nowhere clearly moved me from that status to completely barking mad, in very short order. I had not yet discovered all the short cuts and direct routes, so our journey was a little longer than it needed to be. And once she saw inside the empty shell which was to be my new home, even the formidable Mme LaC was almost lost for words.

She was going straight back, after we'd unloaded the gates and the furniture; I was staying the night to camp out and have another play with my new toy, my little grottage. We'd stopped on the way at a very good bakery and I'd bought us delicious '*croquets aux amandes*', a crunchy, thick, hard almond biscuit from Algeria. I always travel with a flask of boiling water ready for a brew so we sat outside the front door on camping chairs and enjoyed our well-earned break and refreshments.

Then Mme LaC was on her way again and Ci and I were left to wander round our new estate and take stock of all that needed to be done before we could move into it. I'd had little time in the past three months to do anything very much, although I had managed to get France Telecom out for a quote for a phone line and internet connection, as well as getting a couple of electricians and a plumber to come and prepare estimates.

There was a ferocious amount of work which would have to be done before I could live there. At the moment, I was relying on the church a kilometre up the road, which had a lavatory – a loo as many Brits call it - and a hand basin. It was also the nearest place with a reliable dongle internet signal so I could access my emails from my laptop. The church was no longer used for worship, being some three kilometres from the town, where the population had drastically reduced in size over the years. Thanks to its facilities, I somewhat irreverently nick-named it St Loo and St Dongle.

Because of my love of camping, I was well equipped with portable camping gas stoves, a spirit stove for winter and another of my new toys, a rocket stove. This amazing device ran on little bits of twig I found lying round my garden and would easily cook me a meal and produce kettles full of hot water for washing up and washing myself.

But even a confirmed optimist like me needed to take a reality check. And the reality was, the grottage was a long way from being habitable. For a start, I had a pair of gates but no gateposts. Although that evening Ci and I were going to sleep in a bed for the first time in the grottage, there were still no ceilings in any of the upstairs rooms.

My mother had been fond of huffing and puffing when the going got tough. Her favourite saying on the subject had always been: 'Mother was it worth it?', to which her mother, who was made of sterner stuff, would always reply: 'Oh get on with it, child!'

So I had better roll my sleeves up and get on with it. And for the bits I couldn't do myself, it was time to find myself a 'man who does'.

Chapter Three
Of Beds and Brushcutters

Sometimes, when I meet someone for the first time, I seem to 'know' things about them which I couldn't possibly know. Not just an assumption based on appearances, just something I feel I already know. The first time I met Patrick, I had exactly that feeling and the word 'paratrooper' immediately sprang into my mind with conviction.

As I was starting to get to know what would be my local area, I'd popped into some nearby shops and studied the boards with adverts on them, to get a feel for what was available. My grottage was situated a short drive from two small towns. The nearest, Olliergues, about four kilometres away, down a very steep hill into a river valley, had a *mairie*, or town hall, as even the smallest of towns has in France, with a library on its ground floor, two cafés, a hairdresser, a butcher, a baker, two banks, a cheese shop and a small supermarket.

The supermarket brand name was one which catches out endless unwary English speakers new to France. When told they can find food at the Petit Casino, they assume they are in for a pleasant evening playing a little roulette whilst enjoying fine wine and *haute cuisine*. In fact they will be pushing a trolley round a tiny supermarket with a depressing selection of instant meals, both dried and deep frozen, with a universally predominant flavour of reconstituted cardboard.

It was in the Petit Casino that I found a card advertising

services which included, somewhat bizarrely, on the same card, both brushcutting and plumbing. Not customary bedfellows.

One thing I was very anxious to get on with was to see just what my extra plot of land across the road from the grottage was like. It was currently so overgrown it was impossible to see what was there. Drastic though it seemed, I decided the best thing was to get someone in with a brushcutter and just cut everything down to ground level. It had clearly not been touched in years, there was nothing there which was rare or which would not regenerate very quickly, I had already checked, so it would be worth the gamble.

I phoned the number on the card and discovered the person in question lived not five minutes from the grottage. I explained what was needed and arranged a time for him to come and give me an estimate. I wanted to give Ci a quick walk before the appointed hour, so I could leave him in the van out of the way, knowing how much he disliked strangers, especially men, so I took him up the track directly opposite just for a ten minute walk and a quick emptying.

When I got back, two minutes before the time we had arranged, there was a rather battered white van parked outside the grottage with a man and two young boys waiting next to it. I had to ask them to sit back in the van whilst I came past with Ci who was by this time beside himself with fury to see invaders trying to infiltrate his property. But once he was safely back in the van, the man and the boys, his two sons, it turned out, were able to get out for the customary round of handshakes.

As soon as I took the man's hand, I thought 'paratrooper'. There was nothing of the military bearing about him. His hair was collar length, curly and had clearly not recently met shampoo in anger. Nor was it his clothes. True, he wore camouflage cargo pants and a khaki fleece, but that was fairly standard wear out in the country - I was actually wearing the same myself. But still the conviction was there, the knowing, not guessing.

The boys were dark skinned and very dark eyed, good looking boys, one about eight with looks that said he would be a heart breaker before too long. The older boy was perhaps twelve, just starting to turn lanky and awkward, like a colt whose legs were growing too fast for his body.

I showed Patrick, as he introduced himself, what needed doing and we discussed a price. I pointed out that I didn't yet live on site so needed someone I could trust who would come and do the job as promised, on the agreed date, to the agreed standard. I hinted that if he did a good job, there would be more work in the offing.

More handshakes all round and he and his boys drove off whilst Ci and I returned to the Pink House.

The move to the grottage was to be yet another new start for me. Not the first time I had moved home on a whim and started again from scratch in an area I didn't know. But now approaching sixty years of age, I hoped this could well be my last ever move, so everything was done with consideration of the inevitable effects of getting older.

The little town close by should provide me with most of what I would need, and with the taxi-firm-owning Alf, from whom I had bought the grottage, living just around the corner from me, if I ever became unable to drive, I could still get to most things.

I had decided that part of the new start would be a brand new bed. Well, in fact, an antique bed frame with a brand new made-to-measure mattress. I already had a couple of ruptured discs in my neck thanks to one horse, as well as a sometimes painful wedge fracture of the thoracic spine, a gift from a stroppy young stallion with too much testosterone. With advancing age, they were not going to get any better so a custom made mattress seemed like a very good investment and should nicely see me out.

Our eccentric friend Goaty had told me there was a young

man in the nearest town to the Pink House who did made-to-measure mattresses. I had already found a very nice old wrought iron bed frame, thanks to Mme LaC, who knew everything and everyone. She had put me in touch with a friend of hers who had the perfect bed frame, a small double, ideal for me, and very inexpensive. A couple of coats of good quality metal paint and I was very pleased with the results.

So off I went down to the bed man and mattress maker in Combronde, thinking it would be a question of giving him the dimensions of the bed frame, picking out a firmness level for a mattress and that would be that.

How wrong I was!

Nothing in the Auvergne happens very quickly. Whenever you go to a shop, or an office or somewhere for an appointment, you have to allow for longer than any such transaction would take in the UK. By the time the handshakes have been done, or the kisses on both cheeks, and the weather has been discussed – the Auvergnats love talking about the weather! - time has gone by and you haven't even got started.

Mattress Man's shop was on the main road through the little town of Combronde, a small, modest shop front set slightly back under an overhang, with a bed and some fabric samples in the window. I stepped inside and into a small office and tiny showroom on the right, with things like duvets, pillows and mattress toppers crammed onto the small shelving displays.

Mattress Man was older than I had thought from Goaty's description, certainly well into his fifties, small and slight. He told me proudly that he had spent three months in England as a youth because his father had told him the best upholsterers in the world were there and sent him to learn his trade.

He also said that as well as hand-making mattresses and other bedding from scratch, he was also an enthusiastic collector of old bed-making machinery and asked if I would like to see some. Now that I no longer had Mother to look after, my time was largely my own, so I agreed, with pleasure, thinking it would be an interesting five minute walk around a few old machines.

Wrong again!

The building itself was fascinating and labyrinthine. Room opened off room opened off courtyard, each one filled with incredible devices whose purpose I could only guess at, until Mattress Man gave his explanations. There were sacks bursting with horsehair and lambswool, and machines to fluff them and extract the dust. Machines for cutting mattresses, for stitching them, for buttoning them. I had no idea how much work was involved or how fascinating it was.

After the tour, which lasted well over half an hour, it was time to talk about my own requirements. Older style continental beds require a *sommier*, a mesh-sprung bed base, as they come with only head and foot boards and the framework to hold a base to support a mattress. I knew my plan to have everything made to measure was going to be costly, but again, I had no idea of how detailed a business I was embarking on.

My expert adviser asked me about my sleeping patterns, and whether I had any thoughts on a metal or a wood *sommier*? Cross struts in wood or rubber? Once he started mentioning the Faraday cage principle, he lost me completely. It was too much like a school general science lesson, at which I had never excelled. I've always dreaded being in a vehicle which was struck by lightning as I knew it was safe inside one but could never remember if the minute you set foot to the ground outside you were instantly carbonised by any retained electrical charge.

Now we were discussing my general health, and my mention of slight allergic asthma was pounced upon as a significant factor. Once again, I decided I would just have to put myself entirely into Mattress Man's no doubt competent hands, go with exactly what he suggested, and hope that it fitted into my budget.

Next came the business of lying down on various mattresses supported on various different *sommiers* until I found the most comfortable. Then we discussed the depth of the mattress, and it was delicately suggested that the height overall was an important factor for getting in and out of bed as the years advanced.

That seemed to be pretty much it to me in my ignorance. But no, Mattress Man informed me that once both *sommier* and mattress were made, he would need to bring both up to the Pink House to check both for the perfect fit on the bed frame. Then and only then, once any adjustments necessary had been made, could I take ownership of my wonderful new bed.

I was so impressed with the whole thing that, swept up on a heady wave of euphoria, I promptly ordered two expensive made-to-measure pillows to go with the mattress. I was thrilled that these would be made out of old-fashioned blue striped ticking, just like the old pillows I remembered from my youth.

My future sleeping arrangements all sorted, it was time to get on with some serious work at the grottage, starting with getting electricity, water and sanitation restored. But first, another weekend visit and the chance to check up on whether or not the paratrooper had been as good as his word and done the brushcutting job on my plot of land.

As soon as I pulled up at the grottage, I could see that he had, and had done a very good job. I could now see exactly what I had in my one thousand two hundred and twenty square metres. Now all the rogue saplings and brush had gone, I could see that the earth was in strange furrows, what in Lincolnshire they call wheelings, where a heavy vehicle had been.

I was later to discover that the last inhabitant, Monsieur Duchet, was not actually the frail old man I had thought but a raging alcoholic who would do anything for a drink and who had eventually collapsed and died just outside the front door, whilst only in his early sixties. Part of his drive for money to buy drink had included selling off all the topsoil from what was now my strip of land. Oh well, just another small problem to be overcome.

'Mother was it worth it?'

'Get on with it, child!'

I'd arranged for Patrick to call round whilst I was there so I could pay him. I told him I was very pleased with his work and asked him about the plumbing services he offered. I had called in a plumber earlier on, showed him exactly what I needed and asked him for an estimate. He never sent one. The nearest he got to it was to phone me wanting to discuss it. Unfortunately for him, he phoned on the day Mother had died so I gave him short shrift and sacked him before I even employed him.

Could Patrick, I asked him, really set to from scratch and install all the plumbing fittings I needed? And would he be available to start quite soon? He assured me he could and would and that I need have no fears, he was not only a qualified plumber but had done his own house entirely. I was welcome to go round for *apéros* one evening to have a look for myself and to meet the rest of his family.

A qualified plumber/handyman/gardener five minutes from my new house? And a no doubt resourceful ex-para to boot, as he confirmed. Could it be too good to be true? It was certainly worth a gamble.

Chapter Four
Sparks Fly

I'd never previously project managed anything on the scale of the grottage restoration, certainly not single-handedly. I was having a bit of a problem getting my head round what needed to be done first: restore the water supply, or sort out the electrics? Install the septic tank before putting in a bath-room?

The English builder I'd found through my accountant had by now done a good job of putting in a floor to the loft space, effectively creating ceilings to help keep in a bit of warmth. Somewhat bizarrely, he'd decided to put the trap door up into the loft inside the linen cupboard in the spare bedroom, so even for someone of my small stature, it was going to be challenging to get up through it, especially carrying anything to be stored up there. I had to get him to move it.

He'd installed absolutely wonderful huge oak pillars and hung my metal gates from them. I'd put in chain link fencing and metal posts round the previously open sides of the property, so the garden, such as it currently was, was now safely dog-proof and Ci could run about to his heart's content whenever we were at the grottage.

Like most of my BIY – Bodge-it-Yourself – it was not pretty, but it was functional. Stringing chain link fencing, I discovered, is not a job best done single-handedly. The tension of mine reminded me of my early knitting attempts when I had to produce a bobble hat to get some badge or another in the Brownies.

I opted for getting the water restored as the next job. The infrastructure was already in place, and there was even a single cold tap in the rather scratched and battered old ceramic sink in the kitchen.

Water authorities in the region are small syndicates. Mine was the rather mystically named Syndicat Eaux de la Faye, the name of a local river, and was situated in the other nearby town, Augerolles, about six kilometres away. An appointment was made, their technician duly arrived with one of those big T-shaped keys to fit down into the inspection chamber where the water meter was – all water is metered here – and with a bit of grunting and straining, he turned on the long-seized stopcock so water was once again flowing in the grottage for the first time in many years.

That evening really did feel as if I had all mod cons. Well, nearly all, since I still relied on the church of St Loo and St Dongle up the road for the use of a lavatory and a dongle signal to connect to the internet. But at the mere turn of a tap, I could have all the cold running water I required, instead of relying on the bottles I had been bringing with me on each visit.

With my trusty rocket stove cranked up and burning all the windfall twigs and branches from around the garden, once my meal was cooked, I could boil up my kettle for a hot wash, and to fill up a flask ready for my morning tea. What luxury!

I'd met my new next-door neighbour on a few occasions. She was pleasant, and we got on well enough. It was always going to be a tricky situation as her father had been born in what was now my house and had wanted to buy it back. He was always perfectly polite, greeting me with the abbreviated local form of 'Bonjour, madame' which sounded rather like 'mem'. His wife, my neighbour's mother, on the other hand, had the look of a tricky one. She had very sharp features and a long pointed nose which gave her a look of someone very interested in everyone else's business. She loved a bit of doom and gloom, too. She'd already peered over the fence at the various pots of plants and bulbs I had brought with me, lovingly hauled from Lincolnshire, to Wales, to the Pink House and now to the grottage. She made scathing comments on the prospects of any of them surviving an Auvergne winter. They had already survived five of them.

Two mornings after my water was switched back on, however, my neighbour was not in the best of moods and it turned out I was inadvertently the cause. Water was welling up through the inspection pit for my water meter, flowing freely under the fence which separated the two properties and making its merry way into her house underneath the front door.

Oops.

It being a Sunday morning, I wasn't too sure what to do, as I didn't for a moment imagine it would be easy to get someone from the water company out. I phoned Patrick for advice, whilst my neighbour kindly and enterprisingly went off down the hill into the hamlet proper – our two houses being set a bit apart from the others - to see if the semi-retired builder round the corner had one of the big key things with which to turn off the water. I was concerned about who would be paying for the spillage of all that metered water, apart from not wishing to flood my neighbour's house.

Patrick assured me the water board were on twenty-four-hour call-out and kindly gave me their number, so I phoned them. To my astonishment, a man was there within ten minutes, with the required key, and soon had it turned off. He had a look at what had happened and reported that in turning the supply back on, his over-zealous colleague had managed to strip the thread on the stopcock so it would have to be renewed. He also assured me that the water board would pay for the leaked water as it was leaking before it passed through the meter so was at their charge, not mine.

As the stopcock and meter were in a small inspection chamber set into a concrete path, I could see it was going to be a sizeable job to fix it. The water board man assured me they would be back within forty-eight hours to do the necessary. So my brief brush with modern convenience had been brief indeed and in the interim, it was back to bottles of water either brought with me from the Pink House or filched from the wash basin up at the cemetery of St Loo and St Dongle.

True to their word, the water board men were back, two days later. Three men with a mini JCB turned up to dig a huge hole and replace the stopcock, so I once more had some mod cons. I had light, too, as well as water, as I'd invested in two small solar kits, designed for camping. Armed with a solar panel, a battery, a transformer and a couple of plug in lights and, taking advantage of the south-facing aspect, I had plenty of solar light in the evening, enough to read by or do odd jobs indoors, and I could also plug in and charge my mobile phone for nothing.

The local people, the Auvergnats, have a reputation for being very thrifty, bordering on the skinflint. I was definitely becoming an Auvergnate with my dislike of paying EDF, the national electricity company, a centime more than I needed to. It wasn't going to be enough on its own though, so I needed mains electricity, and sooner, rather than later.

I'd had estimates from two local electricians, both quite a bit more than I had hoped to pay but so similar in price that I had to accept their quotes were about the going rate. The whole thing needed to be started from nothing as all the old wiring was no longer up to standard. I also discovered there were now a lot of bizarre regulations which meant I was obliged to have a television aerial point installed in every bedroom, despite me being vehemently opposed to televisions in bedrooms, as well as telephone points everywhere.

I'd chosen one of the electricians, the most local, although neither of them filled me with great enthusiasm. Patrick had now started work on ripping out old fixtures and fittings and was starting on work to dry-line all the walls with plasterboard, heavily insulated behind. I had learned early on that I could trust him completely, so he knew where a spare key was hidden and could let himself into the grottage to get on with his work even when I wasn't there. Not that there was anything in the house yet so I could have left it unlocked. Any passing burglars might perhaps have left me a donation of something when they saw how empty it was inside.

We synchronised operations so that the electrician I'd chosen – let's called him Fabien – could be running all his cables, in their colourful plastic casing, at the same time as Patrick was putting in his pipework for the shower room and kitchen, and then the whole lot could be concealed behind the plasterboards.

My trust in Patrick extended to money matters. I had to confess early on that my slight dyscalculia made me a complete bozo with figures, in any language, although that was obvious the first time Patrick and I were discussing materials needed. I found it was easier just to give Patrick the cash and let him go and get what was needed. I also opened an account at the local builders' merchants, so he was never held up by shortage of materials as I was still only visiting about once a week.

Patrick was from the south-eastern department of le Var, between Marseille and Nice, where the accent is very different to that of the Auvergne. Counting in French always presented me with a problem but mentally translating Patrick's 'ven-senk' into *vingt-cinq*, pronounced locally as 'van-sank' always gave me pause for thought.

As invited, I had been to his house to meet the rest of his family and see the really lovely work he had done on restoring it. I had already given him the green light to do the tiling in my kitchen and shower room based on what I had seen and he was doing a superb job. He was a real perfectionist and took it as a personal affront that nothing within my grottage was in a straight line and that my motto was always 'do whatever is quickest, simplest and most economical.'

Apéros had been an interesting experience. I often have great difficulty explaining to the French that I don't drink, no, not even a glass of wine because yes, that really is alcohol too! It's not that I don't like it or don't approve. It's just that for some reason my body doesn't seem to want me to drink any more. It's probably the result of a fairly debauched youth as a young journalist in Manchester. Luckily, I discovered, Patrick was unable to drink either, due to an illness, so for once I didn't feel too left out. Explaining that I choose not to eat meat, however, was always difficult. Just as well there was plenty of delicious local cheese available. Although I'm not technically a vegetarian, I am close and it's a concept which is still in its infancy in many parts of rural France. On many occasions when I've mentioned not eating meat, in both France and Corsica, I've been offered *jambon blanc*, boiled ham, and been given incredulous looks when I've pointed out that it, too, is meat.

Patrick was also brilliant at making suggestions which I would never have thought of, for little features to make the most of the existing layout of the property. Hence the shower room now boasted some beautifully tiled shelves in a little alcove which would otherwise be dead space. Thanks to him, too, to make the kitchen authentically old and rustic, there were now tiled work surfaces with shelves and storage underneath which I planned to screen with pretty gingham curtains, gingham being called Vichy in French, after the seat of the infamous wartime French State of Marshal Philippe Pétain.

The first time I visited my building site when both Patrick and Fabien the electrician, were working there at the same time, I could have cut the tension, and particularly the latent testosterone, with a knife. Patrick was usually mild-mannered and so quietly spoken I often had to ask him to speak up or to repeat himself.

He and I stepped outside to have a discussion in private, leaving Fabien to play with his coloured wires. Patrick's speech was peppered with '*putain*' (bloody hell) every other word and it was clear he was not at all impressed with Fabien. When I looked at the progress, or lack of it, I had to agree with him. Plug sockets were dotted about in a somewhat haphazard fashion, although I had left a diagram of where they were to be installed. Where I had marked two in the same location, instead of installing a double socket, or even two very close together, Fabien had put two with a gap of several centimetres between them. Absolutely nothing was straight or level, and I could see how infuriating that would be for Patrick's meticulous tiling.

I was already not best pleased with Fabien as when I had arrived, I found him smoking in my house, without ever having asked. Worse, when I immediately asked him not to, he reverted to small-boy-in-playground mode and said: 'Well Patrick does it!'

Patrick had asked, on our first encounter, if he could smoke and I said no. I have a slight but genuine allergy to tobacco and its smoke, which makes me cough and wheeze. Patrick smoked roll-ups and he would often roll one inside the house, especially when it was windy or wet outside, but always took it outside to smoke.

I was about ready to sack Fabien on the spot but he held all the cards. When you accept an estimate in France, you sign it to say 'read and approved' and it becomes a binding contract. If I decided to sack Fabien now, I could well find myself having to pay the full cost of his quote, which I certainly could not afford to do.

I had set him what seemed to me to be a realistic time-scale to finish the work in my very small grottage. I had explained that it was essential to have it all finished by the second week in July when my best friend Jill would be making her annual visit and we planned to spend it at the grottage. I also pointed out how much the lack of electricity was holding up other works as without it, Patrick was struggling to do many of his jobs, although the very kind English builder had lent us his generator without charge.

Fabien whined and whinged and said he wanted access to the keys so he could come and go and do the work whenever it suited him. In no uncertain terms, I told him that was simply not going to happen. He was not a particularly pleasant character, tall and thickset, who seemed to dwarf my house, with its very low ceilings. He wore his jeans so low-slung any teenager would have been impressed. He also smelled as if he was a stranger to soap.

He clearly did not like having his fortune told by a small and slight woman, and an English one, to boot. But the simple fact was that we were stuck with one another, so I spelled it out for him as clearly as I could. When I picked up Jill from the airport in Clermont-Ferrand on the eleventh of July and brought her back to the grottage, I expected her to be dazzled, literally, with the new lights and electrical fittings.

I also expected her to be able to take a hot shower after her journey, as Patrick had by now more or less completed the shower-room and very nice it looked too, with its beautiful blue tiling. So all that was needed was for Fabien to pull his finger out and get on with connecting up all his coloured wires which were currently in a bit of a bugger's muddle, as Mother would have said, and get it all connected up to the mains and approved by EDF.

Too much to ask for?

Chapter Five
Getting SPANCed

The grottage was starting to look positively twentieth century, although it still had a bit of a way to go to catch up into the twenty-first. There was a smart, beautifully tiled shower room, with cold running water which was currently just trickling away down my sloping land into the next field, as did the water from the kitchen sink. There was no problem with that since I only ever used green, eco-friendly products which would cause no damage. The loo could not be used yet because of the absence of a septic tank.

It was time for a visit from the dreaded SPANC, the *Service Public d'Assainissement Non Collectif*. In other words, the sanitation board in charge of non-mains domestic sewage disposal, which would be the case for the grottage as there was no mains drainage for miles around.

Of course English-speakers are always in hysterics at the name and pronounce it as Spank, although the joke doesn't work in French, so the French probably regard it as yet more proof of the inherent insanity amongst the English.

Patrick and I had already discussed various options and locations for a septic tank but ultimately, it would be SPANC who would tell us what we must install and exactly where we must install it. We knew that it would be tight for a septic tank, which, due to modern regulations, needed huge areas of filter beds between the main tank and where any water discharges off the property. But we thought it could probably be done and had been looking at various options.

I instinctively knew my neighbour was the bearer of bad news when one day, whilst exchanging pleasantries over the fence as we often did, she started stroking my arm and calling me '*ma pauvre dame*', poor lady. She was clearly her mother's daughter as she did seem pleased to be able to impart the bad news she had for me.

Did I know, she asked, that the water main for the nearby village, lower down in the valley, passed right through the middle of my property? And did I realise that that was going to severely restrict the possible places I could have a septic tank installed?

No, I did not, and had Alf and Bert, the vendors from whom I had bought my property, been anywhere around, I might possibly have had to be restrained from flinging myself at them and biting their ankles in a way to rival my dog Ci.

Patrick's reaction was predictable and involved several *putains* and a few *bordel de merdes,* roughly equivalent to 'for f*ck's sake'. He said I would have to contact the water board again to come and identify exactly where the water main was buried, before the SPANC visit, so that we would know what our options were.

It was time to bring in my secret weapon. For reasons I don't profess to understand, I can dowse for water. A friend one day handed me a pair of bent, thin copper rods and told me to have a go, which I did, and it worked. Cynics say it is no more reliable than a random method of, say, throwing tennis balls. There would be a roughly equal number of false positives. Only I've never had a false positive. If there's water, my rods take on a life of their own and cross over one another. Otherwise they remain motionless and refuse to budge.

The water board were due the next day, no doubt with very highly technical sonar equipment for locating the water main. Just for fun, I got my rods out and had a wander round the patch of land which I optimistically called my garden, as one day I hoped it would be filled with cottage garden plants instead of grass and nettles.

I got several unequivocally positive readings, which I mentally noted, and which gave me a roughly straight line from top to bottom of my garden, slightly on an angle and, of course, going right through where we had planned to put the septic tank. It would remain to be seen if my findings agreed with those of the experts from the water board.

The man who came was the same one whose over-enthusiasm had resulted in the stripped thread on the old stop-cock. We did the ritual hand-shaking and weather discussion, then I explained that we needed the precise location of the water main before the imminent visit from the man from SPANC.

He went back to his van for his hi-tech equipment, and returned carrying an identical pair of bent, thin copper rods to mine. Just as I had, he wandered back and forth, getting positive readings in exactly the same places and, like me, getting no false positives at all.

Having found the approximate line of the water main, he did, however, dig a small pilot hole and then bring out his clever sonar equipment to pinpoint exactly its location and plot its course across my land with little wooden markers. Both our copper rodding efforts had produced a completely accurate and identical result.

So now it was time for Mr SPANC's visit, and I had arranged for Patrick to be there, as the plan was for him to install whatever septic tank we would be allowed to put in. Once the problems had been highlighted by my helpful neighbour, I'd started looking online for our options and discovered all sorts of incredible mini sewage treatment plants for domestic use in similar circumstances.

Incredible in performance and, of course, incredible in price, coming out at almost twice the figure I had budgeted for, thinking a simple septic tank would do the job. I'd printed out several technical specifications to show to Mr SPANC. One in particular had attracted my interest as the firm was from Luxembourg, home of my late grandmother and a whole collection of cousins and second cousins. The system in question was marketed through an English company, who assured me that it was completely up to the required specifications, was on the SPANC approved list and that there would be no problem with its installation within a Regional Nature Park, as the grottage was in one.

Mr SPANC was having none of it. No filthy foreign sewage treatment plants for him. And certainly not one from Luxembourg via England. *Non, non et non.* It was not on his list, so I could not have it. He did confirm that we would need to put in a *micro-station d'épuration*, a full purification plant, and he gave us a list of the ones which were approved and also, helpfully, a list of local suppliers.

Although Patrick had never installed one before, he had read through all the specifications of every model we were considering and was confident he could do it, but he would need a man with a JCB to come and dig the holes, which would have to be enormous. Luckily he was on reasonably good terms with the semi-retired builder who lived round the corner. He seldom took on any work for anyone these days and had refused to do some jobs for my neighbour.

Patrick said he was notoriously difficult to get on with and his labourers seldom lasted long with him as he worked at a punishing rate which he expected them to match. Also he never took breaks for anything, certainly not for coffee or cigarettes.

Older houses in this area tend to be stone built with a rendering of *pisé* or rammed earth, rather like old-fashioned cob houses in the UK. The modern trend is for *crépi*, which is rough-cast or pebble-dash, usually in a pale pinky-terracotta shade. The builder had done the *crépi* on Patrick's house for him and the two had survived the experience without coming to blows.

I, meanwhile, was dispatched to source one of the units we would be allowed to install by SPANC, and in particular to find one from a supplier near enough who would deliver without it increasing the already formidable cost.

Some were plastic, some were concrete. From an eco point of view, I was not wild about either option. But I definitely wanted something that would last as I didn't fancy going through the whole procedure again in my lifetime. It was going to involve a very large hole, and was the main reason I had not yet made a start on creating the garden which I was itching to make.

I'd bought some plants in tubs with me for a bit of portable random colour and fragrance until I could get them into the ground. One day in late spring when I pulled up at the grottage for another little visit, I was bowled over by the most incredible heady fragrance and I couldn't imagine what it could be.

I'd originally seen the grottage in August so this was my first experience of spring there, and for a moment, I couldn't think which of my plants in tubs was capable of such an exquisite scent. Then I realised it was the magnificent huge broad-leaved lime trees in the next field which towered over my property. They were absolutely smothered in tiny blossoms whose incredible smell was quite out of proportion with their size.

As the temperatures rose, the trees would be absolutely covered in honey bees, so many that their hum was audible from quite some distance away. I absolutely loved those trees! Even on stormy days when they swayed perilously in strong winds, well within reach of crashing through my roof.

I was absolutely outraged one day when an elderly lady was walking past, saw me pottering in my garden and stopped to chat. She said what a nice spot I had and what a beautiful outlook, but what a shame about those tall trees which shaded my land. How different we all are!

But until the formidable hole was dug for my new sewage treatment plant, there was no point at all in doing anything with the garden, and in fact there was no time to do so, with so much else to be done.

In fact, two considerable holes were going to be needed, as the treatment plant we had chosen consisted of two huge concrete tanks, each with two chambers. Sewage entered the first chamber and the overspill moved from one to another of the subsequent ones, over a filter system which was constantly aerated by a pump. The resulting water was of such purity that it could be perfectly safely discharged, through a filter bed of stones, into the next field to soak away or to make its way down to the nearest ditch.

And therein lay another problem. The air pump ran on electricity. The stuff which I did not yet have. The thing which, with Fabien's current rate of progress, I was beginning to think I may never have.

His visits to the property were sporadic, to say the least. Patrick was furious as it was holding up his work. He could not finish installing his plasterboard until all the electrical wires, in their colourful casings, were in place. Fabien was also responsible for putting in the telephone points and I was getting very annoyed about that. I was already paying a monthly rental package for telephone, television and internet, none of which I could use, without electricity.

One of his many excuses, whenever I called at the grottage unannounced to find out what, if any, progress he had made, left me momentarily speechless, though not for the reasons he imagined. I knew from Patrick that Fabien had not been near the place for two weeks, and it showed in the lack of any work done.

When I tackled him about the further delays, he explained he had been unable to work because of his *insolation*. Now the French word *insolation* actually means sunstroke, not insulation as one might logically think, which is *isolation*. I was desperately trying to wrack my brains to work out why being insulated was a bad thing for an electrician.

And so we went on, with endless excuses for lack of work and endless delays and frustrations. Jill's annual visit was getting closer and I was still hoping against all hope that for the week we had planned to stay at the grottage, we were going to have all mod cons in place, including electricity.

Chapter Six
Let There Be Light

Jill has been my best friend since the mid 1980s. I first met her when she came as a customer to the riding centre I had in West Wales in those days. We became good friends, bezzy mates. She is the person I would contact in a crisis, safe in the knowledge that, no matter what the time of day or night, she would somehow arrive on my doorstep first, then ask what the problem was.

We have been on countless holidays together and shared numerous mad adventures, such as sharing a badly leaking tent on a trail ride in Wyoming's Washakie Wilderness, and squashing up close for warmth under an inadequate bivouac in a very rainy Welsh forest on a back-packing trip on horse-back.

I'd also helped her to find her first horse, a very feisty little dun mare called Pearl, more affectionately known as the Old Witch for her complete inability to tolerate fools. I sometimes used to compete on Pearl in show jumping, when Jill was not able to herself. I was always under strict instructions not to win things as that would effectively qualify Pearl out of the novice classes in which Jill liked to compete.

One Sunday we were all at a show and Jill had jumped in an early class but had to leave early to go 'quaking' as we all rather irreverently called the Quaker meetings she attended. I changed the rider's name to mine for the novice class and made my usual promise not to win it, which was well within Pearl's scope.

In fact having qualified with an extremely easy clear round, looking at the jump-off course and the competition, I was wondering how I could convincingly not win on a mare as fast and as clever as Pearl. It seemed the best course of action would be to pretend to forget the jump-off course, hesitate, lose valuable seconds and set time which could easily be beaten.

I'd underestimated just how clever Pearl was. Although she, unlike me, had not seen the jump-off course written up on the board, she clearly had a pretty good idea of which way we should be heading. When I took a pull to slow her, as if hesitating over direction, she took an even bigger pull back and set sail on her way. I practically had to ride head-first into the wall of the indoor school to slow her enough to ensure we were not placed.

And you thought it was only cricket matches and horse racing which were rigged!

Since I'd moved to France, it had become a yearly tradition, to which I looked forward enormously, for Jill to come and spend a week of her annual holidays with me. We'd had some great times. When Mother was still alive, I used to save up all my R&R (days off) by not having any for weeks then taking them all at the same time when Jill came, so we could go away camping.

Jill's strong point is that she never, ever complains. If we had scorching sun or torrential rain, she just accepted it all stoically and we always had fun.

This time, of course, I had no ties with looking after Mother, and I now had a place of my own in which to entertain her. Still a somewhat rudimentary place, admittedly, but habitable for our needs.

I was still hoping against hope that Fabien would finally get his act together and have the electrics sorted out in time for the deadline I had given him, and kept reminding him of. But then I discovered an even bigger delay than I had anticipated.

Electrical installations in France need a certificate from the *CONSUEL, Comité National pour la Sécurité des Usagers de l'Électricité,* the national body for consumer electrical safety, before they can be put into operation. Fabien kept telling me that with summer approaching, it was impossible to get an appointment with the *CONSUEL* for weeks, so we would struggle to meet the deadline.

French summer holidays are absolutely sacrosanct. Especially in the rural areas, they are almost religiously observed, and it is nothing to find businesses closed for a few weeks. If it's the baker, arrangements are usually made for bread to be available from another source for most small communes. But for other businesses, it's just tough. You want a haircut? Or to buy some flowers? Even to go out to dinner? Sorry, we're on holiday, you can't.

Always the optimist, I thought that perhaps if I phoned the *CONSUEL* myself and explained my desperation to get power on so I could move into my own house, I might get somewhere. Especially if I played the 'white-haired old lady living in the middle of nowhere' card.

Only when I phoned them, the real reason for the delay became clear. According to them, no *CONSUEL* visit had been requested by Fabien, the useless lump of lard, despite him telling me on numerous occasions that the only remaining delay was their visit which would be weeks away.

So Jill would be arriving not to the nearly completed but still a bit rustic house she doubtless imagined, but to one which was going to be pretty much as basic as a camping holiday. Still, we'd both survived worse and, as always, I had a cunning plan.

St Loo would provide us with washing facilities and a lavatory pretty much when we needed it and if it was hot enough, which it might well be in early July, a cold shower would be quite pleasant, rather than a penance. I also had a little solar shower for camping trips, basically a black plastic pouch which would heat up water when left in the sun.

Not far from the grottage was a Dutch-owned camp-site, whose owners were well integrated locally, fluent French speakers, whose children went to the local school. I went to see them to ask, if I paid to put a tent there, without needing to sleep in it, could Jill and I then come and use their showers and also have a dip in their small swimming pool?

When I explained what had happened, they were delighted to help and refused to take the full price of a pitch, instead just taking a modest sum to cover our showering and swimming. And as we always liked to have a little trip away somewhere during Jill's visits, I booked us both in at my friend Christine's B&B where we could also have hot showers.

So that it would be less work for my brother whilst I was away, I was putting two of the collection of cats we had acquired at the Pink House into a cattery for the week. HRH Princess Freddie, the little Siamese cross, was a difficult customer at the best of times. She had decided she did not like to be handled by anyone except me and that was only under sufferance. There was also now a sweet little stray who had arrived and presented us with three kittens, all of which I had luckily managed to re-home.

Little Black Blaze, or Bibi, for short, was an adorable cat, so smiley and purry, but she did like to wander about and was so used to coming when I called her, I wasn't sure if she would know my brother well enough to come to his call. I worried about the lethal road in front of the Pink House which had already claimed two of our cats' lives.

So on the morning Jill's flight was due to arrive at Clermont-Ferrand, I loaded cats in cages into the van with Ci, filled up my little camping trailer with all the emergency provisions and equipment we might need for roughing it at the grottage and set off to collect Jill. I stopped at the cattery on the way to unload the cats and was rewarded by one of HRH's famous withering sapphire blue stares as I left her there with Bibi.

Jill's flight was in well on time and I drove her back by not the most direct route but the one which gave her the best first glimpse of my new home.

Of course, there was no light at the grottage. Well, apart from my little camping solar panels, which gave us enough light to read by. There was also no television, no telephone, no hot water. But the weather was glorious. We sat outside the front door with the rocket stove going like a good 'un and cooked and brewed up and heated water to wash in. We sat and chatted till the sun sank in a haze of pinky-orange splendour behind the chain of volcanoes, and I could see that Jill really got it, and knew why I felt I had found my special forever home.

We spent a couple of days just exploring the glorious scenery all around, walks with Ci, picnics, cook-outs on the rocket stove. We invited Patrick and his family around for *apéros*. Theoretically drinks and an appetiser before the main meal, in this area at least, the appetisers I've been served would make a full evening meal for me, with a doggy bag for a packed lunch the following day.

I wanted to introduce Patrick and his family to some English food so Jill had kindly brought over tasters of various British cheeses. That was always going to be tricky for a country which prides itself on its cheeses and has probably as many as there are days in the year. However, they really enjoyed 'proper' English Cheddar, instead of the bright orange plastic stuff found on a certain brand of burger, and were also quite taken with unusual taste fusions like Stilton with apricots. But the biggest culture shock they tried and really liked was Branston pickle!

We decided to take the scenic route on our way to Christine's for our little visit, to see some of the local Livradois-Forez region, with its varied scenery. A lot of it was heavily wooded, but would occasionally open out into wide, lush valleys, dotted with various breeds of cattle, including the glorious Auvergnat breeds, Salers, with their rich mahogany coats and impressive lyre-shaped horns, and the more rare Ferrandaises, usually red and white.

I'd been browsing guide books and maps of the area and, as we often did, we were heading for what was marked as a viewpoint, in the middle of nowhere. There was supposed to be a rocky outcrop, with some religious statue or another at its summit, which afforded spectacular views of the surrounding countryside.

We found the area in which it was meant to be situated, and by asking in a nearby village, managed to find the rough cart track leading up to it. My Opel Combo van, affectionately known as Blue, was used to tackling such challenges and made little protest.

The track ended in a very small clearing in a wood, with no sign of either rocky outcrop nor religious statue, just what looked like a partially underground reservoir. I was just turning the van round to park so we could get out and explore when a passing walker flagged me down and asked if I knew one of the rear tyres was flat.

Oops!

Not to worry, both Jill and I are fairly resourceful and had changed many tyres in our time. We needed to get Ci out of the van so I could get at the spare wheel, which was under the floor, so Jill took custody of the dog whilst I set about removing the damaged tyre.

As I was doing so, another car pulled up into the very small parking area. As if this were not coincidence enough, with so little traffic about, it was a British registered car, with a Welsh sticker on the back.

An older couple got out, the man certainly well into his seventies. He immediately asked kindly, in laborious schoolboy French, if I needed help, and was very relieved when I answered in English and said that was kind.

He had a much superior car jack to mine so got that out and set to work raising Blue and getting the damaged tyre off. We chatted as he worked. His wife said they now lived in Wales, as did Jill, but were originally from Stockport, my home town. It was such an improbable coincidence that to put it in a work of fiction would be to be disbelieved. But it was true enough.

The man got the old wheel off with not too much difficulty, but then the problems began. The wheel studs had somehow got a bit out of alignment. So when it came to offering up the spare wheel, the studs didn't quite line up with the holes, no matter how we wiggled the wheel about.

Worse, in his enthusiasm to help, our new friend managed to shift things so the margin of error went from a couple of nths to a good few centimetres. So we were marooned in the woods with a three-wheeled van.

Luckily my van is always fully equipped for emergencies, so there was a tent, bedding, food, a gas stove and goodness knows what else, should the worst come to the worst. But I did have full breakdown cover as part of my insurance package. All I had to do was phone for them to send out a breakdown man who doubtless, with all the right equipment, would be able to sort things out.

Mortified at having made things worse rather than better, our British friends drove off, leaving us alone in the woods.

I phoned my breakdown service and got an estimated call-out time of two hours. I then sent Christine a text to explain the situation and to say we had no idea what time we would arrive for the evening meal we had booked and our nice bedroom with welcome hot showers.

In the meantime we set off for a walk with Ci and did manage to find the rocky outcrop, complete with statue of the Blessed Virgin, and the view was certainly worth the effort. As is often the case with volcanic rock outcrops, it was a magnet for butterflies, who presumably come to seek the minerals in the rock. We saw all sorts of sizes, shapes and colours, yellows, blues, fritillaries, and plenty of the big and bumbling swallowtails.

Then it was back to the van for a cup of tea from the trusty flask which always travelled with me, and to wait for the breakdown man to ride to our rescue on his white charger. Or whatever means of transport he was going to be able to manage to bring up the not very wide and rather rough track in the wild woods..

It was a long wait. A few walkers passed us, as did a few riders on horses and several cyclists, whom Ci wanted to kill. Then we saw a lone walker coming up the pedestrian track, rather than the vehicular one, who didn't seem particularly well equipped for hiking in rough country. This, it turned out, was our knight in shining armour. On foot, without his recovery vehicle, and without even a toolbox in his hand.

Bless him, he had stopped his truck earlier than I had told him to when he had phoned for directions so saw only the narrow footpath up to the summit. But to his credit, he had at least used his initiative in leaving his truck at the bottom then coming up on foot to do a recce to see what the problem was and what he could do about it.

He seemed incredibly impressed that we had managed to drive the van up to where we were, although compared to some of the places I had taken poor old Blue, it was a walk in the park.

It was a matter of minutes for him to tinker about with my tools, do a bit of wiggling of the wheel, then get the spare on and pumped up to a decent pressure. He showed me a clever trick in case the same thing ever happened to me again, which I promptly forgot, and then he asked plaintively if I could drive him back to his truck. I willingly did, grateful as I was that he had not taken one look at the access and driven away. This meant leaving poor Ci with his Auntie Jill, no doubt worrying he had once more been abandoned, as he had when he first finished up in the refuge from which I got him.

The recovery man was even more impressed when I drove him down the track. I think he was a bit of a townie who would not have ventured to take any vehicle up such a rough route. I'm sure he dined out for weeks afterwards on the tale of the two completely mad English ladies and their van broken down on top of a volcanic rock in the middle of nowhere.

After such an adventure, the lovely hot showers which awaited us at Geoff and Christine's, followed by a delicious supper all together round the big table, were all the more welcome.

On the morning of Jill's return flight, I thought I had arranged with Patrick to come at a slightly later time than usual to start work on the house, so we could have a leisurely breakfast together before she left.

Something had clearly been lost in the translation as, whilst we were still sitting outside eating, he turned up ready to work. His job for the day was to cut out the old and very woodworm-ridden staircase to make way for the smart new made-to-measure one his carpenter neighbour had made for me,. So it was going to be not only a noisy job, but one which meant we needed to bring everything down from upstairs which we were likely to need. Once Patrick had finished chainsawing, there would be no access to the upper floor, short of a ladder, until the new staircase was fitted.

So slightly earlier than planned, and in a bit more of a rush, it was time to take Jill to the airport for her flight and then for me to head back to the Pink House once more, picking up the cats on the way. Still with no electricity and no sanitation, I was no nearer being able to move into my own home.

Chapter Seven
The Tea Party

I was gearing up for another visitor. My dear friends of nearly forty years, Bob and Peg, had finally decided, now both in their nineties, that their days of foreign travel were over. But their eldest son Bobby had so much enjoyed his visits to France with them that he wanted to come again on his own, to see how things were progressing with the grottage.

The very good news on the progress front was that finally, nearly two months behind schedule, the electricity supply had got the all clear. I would soon be able to use the telephone and the internet, though I still planned to use my solar camping kits for light much of the time. As it was free, it seemed stupid not to.

I'd moved most of my furniture into the grottage now as I had been spending every R&R visit there wielding a paintbrush, painting over all the plasterboards Patrick had installed.

My brother is exceedingly good at shopping and actually likes doing it, whilst I hate it. Whenever he went back to the UK, I gave him a list of things I could not easily get in France and he always came back with brilliant bargains.

I always prefer to shop locally when I can but it has to be said, paint in France is not only expensive, it is generally pretty dire. It takes far more coats to achieve decent cover than even the cheap UK paint from the big DIY stores. So I got my brother to bring back large quantities of trade quality paint to slap about all over everywhere.

I wasn't too fussed about colours, within a certain palette, so I gave him *carte blanche* to find what he could. There was much texting and many phone calls to check that what he had found in the bargain bins would be suitable, and I must admit to a certain reticence about the idea of a Banana Dream bedroom, but it all worked really well and looked fabulous.

The previously deep turquoise sitting room, which looked like something from a hippy squat, was now a warm, neutral cream, which made it appear lighter and look much bigger. The kitchen, which had been the sort of bilious green favoured in hospital corridors, was now light and fresh, in a shade called Appledore. I'd gone with that, too in my bedroom as it had the tiniest hint of pale green about it which worked perfectly with my old *art deco* green rug.

The guest bedroom was now beautifully bright and sunny in Banana Dream, and as I had found two lovely vintage throws in yellows and browns, with my high-sided pine beds in there and some antique pillow cases, it looked really inviting.

The shower room was white, to let the beautiful blue tiles take centre stage. Patrick had introduced me to the most wonderful tile warehouse not far away, which claimed to be the largest in France. It was certainly very unusual in that it was open every day of the year, including Sundays, and even Christmas Day, a rarity for any type of home improvement store in France.

There is a persistent urban myth that France is a Catholic country. It isn't, it's entirely secular. Nevertheless few shops are open on a Sunday, certainly not in the rural areas. It's not for any religious reasons, it's simply to give the shop-keepers an essential day off each week.

As well as their main range of floor and wall tiles of all sorts, the tile place also had an enormous hangar-like building full of seconds and end of line items. It was a wonderful place for a bargain and I had found beautiful Italian tiles at a fraction of the price they would have cost me in a *décor* shop.

In the end I'd decided to splash out and pay a removals firm to move my bigger furniture items from the Pink House to the grottage. There wasn't all that much of it and I could probably have hired a van or got Mme LaC to help me with it. However I wasn't sure how some things, like the *sommier* for my bed, were going to fit round the very tight turn from the steep narrow staircase into my bedroom. So I decided it was worth shelling out to get the experts to do it.

When I saw how much of a juggling act it was even for them, I was highly delighted that I had done so. At least this time my big mahogany dining table, which had made many moves with me in the thirty-odd years I had had it, was able to go in relatively easily through the front door. The poor old table had been pushed and hauled in and out of several very small cottage windows in its time, when there was no other way to get it in or out.

There were only two rooms downstairs in the grottage, and the kitchen was roomy enough to accommodate the big table as my workstation for my copywriting work. The sitting room would be kept for relaxing and watching television, just as soon as I had satellite dishes installed. Being as French as possible was all very well, but I still needed my fix of Coronation Street!

My next visitor, Bobby, or YB as I always called him (Young Bobby was in his sixties, so-called to distinguish him from his father, Bob Senior, who was in his nineties) was due to visit mid September, and I was very nearly, but not yet quite, ready to move permanently into my grottage.

He would come first to the Pink House, then spend a few days at my grottage by himself at first, later joined by me, before heading back home. He was driving over in his little Suzuki car which I disparagingly called half a car, but which would give him some independence at the grottage, as I would not be there all the time he was. I still had things to sort out at the Pink House before finally making the move.

YB was particularly keen to visit the area near the grottage because of its cutlery capital town, Thiers. His mother Peg's maiden name was Thier, and she was apparently distantly related to a former French president, Adolphe Thiers. As a birthday treat for YB, I arranged for him to go to a workshop in Thiers where he could make his own pocket knife, engraved with the Thier name.

I love a tea party! My mother was the same, any excuse to get out the best china cups and bake cakes and scones. So I decided to combine YB's visit with my first official tea party at the grottage.

I invited Patrick and his wife, their two sons, Thomas and Dorian, and older teenage daughter, Julie, the English builder who'd done the early work on the place, with his wife and their two small children, and my English friends Geoff and Christine, making thirteen in total. I decided that as we wouldn't actually all be sitting at table together, I would take a risk on the old superstition.

There were a couple of minor hitches to the plan for a tea party. The weather was set fair, so we could safely be outside in the garden-to-be. But we had now taken delivery of the sewage treatment plant which was to be installed. So the garden was temporarily host to two very large concrete tanks, just plonked down side by side on the grass, not exactly a decorative feature.

Also there was the slight problem over the lack of a loo. The men, especially the French ones, would have no problem using a tree in the corner of the garden, but it might be a bit tricky for the ladies.

Not for nothing do my French friends nickname me *le scout*, which is pronounced in French as 'scoot'. 'Be Prepared' has always been my motto! I also have an impressive collection of tents, considering there is just one of me; four, at the last count.

A portable chemical loo of the sort used in boats and caravans, inside my double-skinned Quechua Base tent, with plenty of room in which to stand up, tucked discreetly away in the corner near the barn, would easily solve the problem of 'facilities'.

As for the concrete tanks, I'd just have to make sure the cakes and scones tasted good enough to stop everyone from looking at the tanks too much.

There was still a bit of work needed before the complete electricity supply could be fully operational, but my friends Geoff and Christine had very kindly lent me a bottled gas cooker, with four rings and a decent oven, and I had my two rocket stoves as well. I would also be able to do some baking at the Pink House in advance of the party.

On the day of the tea party, YB was put in charge of feeding the rocket stoves for boiling up water and, inevitably, they provided a focal point for the menfolk to gather round and discuss. They were still something of a novelty, and of course, boys and their toys – they all had endless fun playing with them.

Playing with fire was tempting for the small children but to distract them from attempting it, I brought out the smallest of my tents. I have a habit of naming many inanimate objects which I use on a regular basis. The tent was called Loppy Lugs.

It was one of the new generation of pop-up tents and was absolutely brilliant. With its bendy carbon fibre tent poles, it could be easily collapsed and put away in moments. But putting it up was truly amazing, and the children loved it. All you had to do was unfasten a restraining strap and whoosh, within two seconds, the tent had erected itself and was ready to use.

In foul weather, I could even throw it out of the back of the van then dive straight into it with my dog. No more getting soaking wet putting up a tent. It could be pegged down with guy ropes and tent pegs but as it was a self-contained double-skin, the combined weight of me and a dog usually held it pretty securely. Best of all, it had large side flaps which could be raised or lowered, just like the ears of a lop-eared rabbit, hence the name, which were blissfully cooling on sultry summer nights.

The children loved playing in it and it kept them safely away from the rocket stoves, leaving the grown-up boys to play with those to their hearts' content.

The tea party was a great success and was, in its way, a formal christening of the grottage. In just over a week's time, the electricity would finally be on, followed very soon by the installation of the sewage treatment plant, so I could at last move in, almost a year after I bought it.

I was planning on bringing two of the cats, HRH and Bibi, with me. Although I'm much more of a dog person than a cat person, those two had rather adopted me. They would have to live in the barn because at close quarters cats give me slight asthma and Ci liked to try to chase them whenever he could. Once they settled in, though, they would soon be able to go out and roam about, and for HRH, this would be for the first time in her life. The road outside the Pink House was so lethal, and she was just not street-wise, so I had never dared take the risk with her.

This would still leave my brother with five cats at the Pink House, more than enough for him to manage. Yet another female cat had turned up there and deposited a litter of kittens a few months earlier. I began to think there was some sort of special cat marking on the gate, like the *patteran* or trail signs used by the Romany gypsies. The one at the Pink House probably said 'gullible English people with more money than sense who will feed any stray cat who turns up here.'

The mother of the Spice Kittens, as I named them, sadly died, as she was very young and in very poor condition, and one of the kittens, Scary Spice, perished on the road whilst still quite young. But that still left Baby, Ginger and Sporty Spice, as well as the old feral tom, Sandy, clearly their father, plus another old black and white tom, Felix.

HRH and Bibi would need time to get to know their new surroundings so, until I was absolutely sure the barn was completely secure to contain them, I was using the base tent inside the barn to house them. They didn't seem to mind their temporary home too much, thankfully. And yes, of course, the Quechua Base tent also had a name – Count Basie. What else?

I had decided that, once I finally moved out of the Pink House and into my grottage, there would be no going back. It held no especially happy memories for me. Left to his own devices, I knew my brother would never be able to manage the upkeep of it as I had done. There was an awful lot of work involved to maintain such a big house and large garden and I could not bear the thought of going back there and seeing the state it would inevitably slide into once I left.

Nor would my brother be visiting the grottage. His two means of transport were not suitable. The little electric Clio, known as the tuk-tuk, did not have the autonomy for the round trip and he would never manage his big motorhome, nick-named the Dingley, on the narrow and twisty roads up to the grottage.

I would keep in touch with him, of course, but from now on, we would in all probability only meet on neutral territory.

Chapter Eight
Meeting the Natives

Ci and I, and the cats, had now taken up permanent residence at the grottage, so it was time to get to know our neighbours. The hamlet in which we now lived had no more than a dozen houses, fairly spread out.

I was gradually getting to know people by sight and of course everyone knew me. It was not every day a lone mad English woman took up residence in such a small community, and Brit ex-pats were still quite a novelty in the area generally.

My new wildlife neighbours were also of great interest to me. On one of my weekend stays at the grottage in summer, whilst sitting outside late at night to watch shooting stars, I'd met a very large and very pale coloured hedgehog, snuffling round the garden and helping with the slug and snail over-population problem.

On our walks around the area, Ci and I had often seen roe deer, their white rump flashes betraying their quiet passage through the woods, as well as occasional wild boar, which we tried to avoid as they can be nasty. There was a lot of hunting in the area. Throughout the hunting season, men with guns would be swarming all over the place in pursuit of all sorts of prey. Despite their best efforts, I still saw plenty of wild-life.

There were lots of foxes, too, and strangely, they, like the red squirrels we often saw in the beech woods, were often very dark indeed, looking almost black from a distance.

The bird life was amazing. Through the seasons I'd seen green, black, lesser and greater spotted woodpeckers. Jays were two a penny. Great flocks of twittering long-tailed tits would often fly by, stopping off in my garden as if to check on the progress of work.

The area was a paradise for lovers of birds of prey, like me. Apart from the usual smaller hawks like kestrels and sparrow hawks, there were all sorts of large birds, from common European buzzards in all colours, from very dark to almost white, to the magnificent short-toed eagles, so large yet capable of hovering motionless over their prey.

As the migrants started to return in spring, I would hear the 'hoop-hoop-hoop' call of the hoopoe, and was thrilled to see flashes of black and yellow, as normally shy and hard to spot male golden orioles fought over territory. There were plenty of cuckoos, too, and very vocal they were. Much as I love birds, after several hours of 'cuckoo-cuckoo' I did sometimes feel like shouting: 'Don't you know the rest of the words?'

Now as autumn was here, the migrants had gone back to their winter quarters, leaving just the hardy native species behind. Blackberries fruited early around the grottage – I'd been picking the first ripe ones in July which was much earlier than I'd ever done in England.

I'd had a bit of an encounter early on with one of the near neighbours who lived just down the hill. Ci did not like men very much, especially coming onto his property, and always barked whenever he saw Patrick, sometimes refusing to be quiet no matter what I did.

The man from down the road came storming up one day, complaining that he could hear the dog barking and it was the same every weekend whenever I visited. Of course his presence, shouting the odds as he was, was the proverbial red rag to a bull, winding Ci up into an absolute frenzy.

I didn't want to fall out with the neighbours before I'd even moved in, so I assured him I would take steps to deal with the situation and tried, whenever possible, to put Ci away in the van when Patrick was about.

One of the things I had been really been looking forward to doing once I moved in was to be able to visit the library. Looking after Mother had been incredibly restricting in that I could not go anywhere when I was on duty with her. On my days off, all I really wanted to do was to escape into the middle of nowhere and chill out.

Now my time was my own, I would be able to do simple things like shop when I liked and go to the library when the fancy took me. My nearest small town of Olliergues had a library in the ground floor of the *mairie*, the town hall, which was open Tuesday and Wednesday afternoons and Saturday mornings. There was also a small market in the town on Saturday mornings, so I was looking forward to being able to go to both on a regular basis.

I decided to go along to the library one afternoon to make enquiries and find out the procedure for becoming a member.

The library was quite small but well appointed, nice and bright and airy. I explained to the librarian on duty that I was new to the area and wanted to become a member. She processed all the paperwork for me, then showed me round.

My favourite genre being crime novels, she took me first to that section. On the way, she proudly pointed out their collection of books in English, perhaps twelve in total. I assured her I only wanted to read in French, being anxious to improve my vocabulary at every available opportunity.

She was incredibly kind and helpful and to be sure I understood, at each section she took me to, she would read aloud to me the label indicating what genre of books it contained. She showed me all round everywhere. It reminded me of my first day at school. I almost expected her to allocate me a peg to hang my coat and a pigeon-hole in which to keep my pencil-case and gym shoes.

As part of my desire to be as green as possible in my new lifestyle, I had decided to invest in an electric bicycle. Because it was always the name I had associated with trips to France in my youth, I chose a Solex. I had very fond memories of riding a Solex on my school exchange visits to France. That was a marvellous old contraption. To start it, you had to pedal away like mad then push a lever to drop the motor onto the front wheel whereupon it took over the work and off you went.

I had originally wanted to get the electric version of the moped. But the man in the shop persuaded me that the bicycle version would better suit my needs. The moped version required registration and paperwork but more importantly, as he pointed out, if for any reason it broke down, it was unusable. With the bicycle version, if the motor should fail, it could still be ridden as a bicycle, albeit a heavy one, and pedalled along.

I was at pains to point out the many hills around where I lived, worried that battery power might not be up to the job, especially as the bike had to be pedalled at all times, even when running on electrical power. He assured me it would be fine, so I bought one and named it Tomato, because of the bright orangey-red of the seat.

A trip to Olliergues with Tomato would be out of the question as there was a very long and quite steep hill down to the town, which would have to be pedalled back up. Even with maximum assistance from the electric motor, it would be a formidable ride for someone like me, who was not by nature a cyclist.

The other nearby town, Augerolles, although slightly further, was actually easier, as there were as many downs as ups in both directions, so it should not be too much of a problem. I had already followed Patrick's advice and registered with the doctor in Augerolles. He told me she was very good but warned me she was so thorough, spending a lot of time on each consultation, that it was not unusual for her to be running up to two hours late for appointments by the end of the morning.

Most towns in this area have a *pharmacie* and both Olliergues and Augerolles had one, so I thought it would be very good and extremely healthy to be able to pedal to the doctor and on to the *pharmacie* to have any prescription I was given filled there. There was also a bakery and a tiny Petit Casino shop in Augerolles, plus a very small market on a Sunday, so I could even do a bit of shopping on the electric bike.

Of course, things don't always turn out quite how you expect when planning an idyllic new lifestyle. Sometimes luck is not altogether on my side with some of my purchases. The electric bike had a display panel which showed how much battery life was available. The panel had to be switched on and illuminated in order for the battery and the motor to communicate with one another. I quickly discovered that sometimes, if I went over even a small pebble in the road, the screen would go blank and the motor would die.

Sometimes just switching off then on again would get it going, but it shook my confidence a bit as, without its motor power, the bike was very heavy going indeed to pedal up any hills, and it was impossible to go more than a few metres in any direction from the grottage without encountering hills.

I took it back to the shop and told them there appeared to be a loose connection. They said they would give it a good looking at and have it ready for me in a couple of days. True to their word, when I phoned back, it was ready for collection.

The shop was on the southern edge of Clermont-Ferrand, so almost an hour's drive for me in each direction to take it and collect it. When I arrived, they told me the battery hadn't been charging properly, so they had replaced it. They told me it might be because I hadn't stored the battery fully charged when not using the bike in bad weather.

I'd started using a phrase when people made remarks which

implied I was some sort of idiot. '*Je suis Anglaise, je ne suis pas bête*', I'm English, I'm not stupid. The instruction book for the bike came in several languages, including English, and I had followed exactly what it said about how to store the battery, which was partially charged, never full or flat.

Of course, changing the battery made no difference at all to the intermittent fault. Any time I went over a small bump, the screen would go blank and the motor would cut out.

The bike became extremely well travelled, though not under its own motor power. It had two more trips back to the shop. Each time I told them there was clearly a loose connection. But what could I possibly know? I was a woman, and English, to boot.

The second time I was issued with a new battery charger. The third time some small electrical component was replaced. Neither solved the problem.

Next Tomato got to go on not one, but two trips to Paris, to the main dealer. The first time they changed some other small electrical component, which made not the slightest bit of difference. The second time they announced they thought there might be a loose connection. No! Why hadn't I thought of that?

They fiddled a bit more. They never did find the particular loose connection which caused the problem. Tomato still randomly cuts out when the fancy takes it, but I've now learned to live with it.

Riding around the lanes and towns is a great way to meet and chat to people, especially as the electric bike is still something of a rarity. Not surprisingly, given the amount of trouble I've had with mine. People often stop to ask about it and admire its fine lines. It is certainly a stylish beast and would be an excellent investment, if it could be relied upon to keep going.

I also added a rigid arm coupling device, for attaching a dog to the bicycle frame, so Ci could come on some trots round the lanes with me and get a bit of exercise.

It was because of a cow on the road one day that I met another of my near neighbours. It happened during one of Jill's visits. We were driving back from Olliergues when we noticed a red and white cow wandering about on the road. The field from which she had escaped was not near to any farmhouse so I wasn't sure to whom she belonged.

One nearby farmer kept his cows in the field next to mine and he would always nod to me as he passed on his tractor. In fact his nod was so deep it was almost like a little bow. I wasn't sure which his house was though, to go and ask him, although I was sure he would know to whom the cow, or rather the heifer, as she was young, belonged.

Jill and I drove around trying to find someone, harder than it sounds in this quiet little backwater. In the end I drove down the hill into the hamlet itself and into the gateway of quite a large farm by the little village pond.

It was such a large house, compared to the others close by, it may originally have been the main farm after which the hamlet was named, the name Le Mas being a southern French word for a farm. As is customary in many of the larger local houses, it had a round tower on the outside, which probably contained nothing but the staircase.

I knocked at the door and a man's head appeared from out of a window at the very top of the tower. We exchanged greetings and I explained why I had called. I couldn't remember the French word for heifer so I just said a young cow.

The man made no attempt to come downstairs to talk to me, we just carried on a conversation with him calling down from the top of the tower and me shouting back up to him. It reminded me rather of the German fairy tale, Rapunzel. He didn't appear too concerned, and said the owner of said heifer would doubtless be along later in the day to check on his cattle and would put her back. I just hoped she didn't get knocked over in the meantime.

I finally met the Bowing Farmer to talk to one warm day when I was pottering about my plot of land across the road from the grottage, experimentally prodding in a few random seeds to see what, if anything, would grow there. The absence of proper top soil may have prevented it from being very productive so I just wanted to do a bit of test planting to find out.

The Bowing Farmer was just about to drive past, saw me there and instead stopped his tractor and came across to chat. He was wearing a check shirt, open over a vest, and possibly the shortest shorts I have ever seen anyone wear without running the risk of a conviction for indecent exposure.

The flapping tails of his shirt didn't quite provide the added cover necessary, and to round off the very fetching outfit, his skinny, knobbly-kneed legs were thrust into the short welly boots which are so popular round here.

I wasn't sure I could carry on any sort of conversation with him without giggling, so after a polite greeting, I carried on pottering in the soil whilst we talked.

He was very quietly spoken and very 'sympa', an all-encompassing term meaning nice and so much more. He was genuinely interested in my plans to try out various exotic grains and vegetables, like quinoa and mashua. And this in an area where the humble parsnip was regarded as an exotic crop and could usually only be found in the rare fruit and veg section of the larger, more cosmopolitan supermarkets.

In the local tradition, he didn't tell me his name nor ask me for mine. He probably knew mine, since names are always displayed on the external letter boxes each house must provide at its boundary, to make postal deliveries much quicker and more efficient. I would have to find out where he lived and go and read the name on his post box since it seemed to breach some sort of local etiquette to ask someone their name if they had not offered it.

Chapter Nine
Breakdown

My trusty Vauxhall Combo van had done sterling work ferrying me about for the past five years. It was a good, solid vehicle, not very glamorous, but extremely functional. There was plenty of room for me and Ci, plus all our camping gear, on our trips away. The little Luton over the cab was a real boon, the ideal stash for sleeping bag, spare clothes and a few bits and bobs.

But lately, it had become an unreliable starter. In fact, more of a non-starter, rather too frequently for comfort. It would usually start with a bump-start but it wasn't always practical to park it on a slope.

I had created a little driveway of sorts to the grottage. It still needed hardcore to level it up a bit and make it more durable, but I could park there rather than on the side of the road. It worked well, except that it sloped the wrong way, down, towards the house, so was no good at all for bump starting.

There was no real problem about parking a vehicle outside my property on the side of the road. Crime was so low in the area I wasn't worried about theft. Even if crime had been rife, no-one would take an old Vauxhall van, or Opel, as the brand is called in France, and certainly not a right-hand drive one. In addition, it was a distinctive royal blue with a big flashing orange roof-bar light, so was very easy to identify.

Once the snows came, though, leaving it on the roadside was hazardous, to say the least. In order to be certain of driving off safely, I liked to leave the two roadside wheels on the tarmac rather than the grass verge, for grip. But the road was narrow and when it was icy, snowy and slippery, I worried about another vehicle sliding into it. Also whenever the snow-plough passed, which was usually several times a day when the weather was bad, really good news in such a small, isolated location, the driver couldn't really be expected to lift his blade for every parked car he passed so poor Blue would often be buried in a snowdrift.

Bump-starting became extremely perilous in the bad weather, too. The van had to be parked facing north as that was the direction of the slope, and after the first few yards, I had a choice of direction. To the left was a steep but relatively short incline down into the hamlet, where Blue tended to build up rather too much speed too quickly for me to be confident of avoiding the houses at the bottom of the slope. Straight ahead, towards Augerolles, was a much better bet as there was a very long but much more gradual descent. But after a few hundred yards, there was a sharpish left hand bend where a ditch always overflowed so it was like an ice rink. If I hit that spot before the motor was running, leaving me without engine braking, there was no way safely to negotiate the bend without sliding into the ditch on the right, or plummeting over a drop down into a stream to the left.

Clearly I couldn't continue without a reliable vehicle, living out in the sticks with non-existent public transport. A couple of local garages had taken a look and made expensive diagnoses. It just was not worth throwing a load of money at an elderly vehicle which did have a few drawbacks.

I'd managed for five years with the right-hand drive but it did present problems and safety issues. Being a van, with no side windows, visibility was sometimes non-existent to the left and it could be extremely dangerous joining a main road from a slip road and being able to see virtually nothing coming. In extreme cases I'd simply had to put on the four-way flashers and the roof bar light and inch my way out blind into the oncoming traffic.

The *péages* or toll booths on the motorway were a bit of a nightmare, too. I had to do some inelegant wriggling over the hand brake and gear lever to lean out of the passenger window to drop my coins in the slot. You are not supposed to get out of the vehicle at the booths to run round and put the money in. Although I didn't often use the motorways, it was a factor to consider, especially as the windows were manual wind, so I would be pulling away from the *péage* trying to wind the passenger window, get back into my seat belt and avoid vehicles merging lanes from both sides of me.

Blue also did not have power steering. I had always managed perfectly well without but I was starting to have problems with my hands and wrists with arthritis and carpal tunnel syndrome. I was already supposed to wear my very fetching 'bondage strapping' night and day, but didn't always. The lady who had custom-made the rigid night straps for my hands, and who suffered with the same conditions herself, said power steering was a must and that I should also consider an automatic.

My brother has always favoured automatics but I dislike them intensely, finding them unresponsive in comparison to a manual and really hating not being able to bump-start in times of need. I was willing to compromise on power steering, but an automatic was a step too far at this stage.

I couldn't remotely afford a new car, although I did for a moment toy with the idea of a Dacia, with its long warranty and free initial servicing, but it was simply beyond my budget, so it would have to be second hand. The price of used cars in France was eye-watering. Vans in particular changed hands for four times or more what they cost in the UK.

The idea of looking for a left-hand drive van in the UK and

getting someone to bring it over for me appealed at first, but the sheer logistics of it were a bit daunting. I would have to bite the bullet and try to find something in France which would suit and which I could afford.

I started trawling the excellent advertising website, *Le Bon Coin*, which is where I had actually found the grottage. For my lifestyle, it needed to be a van or an estate car at least, roomy enough for me to sleep in on my camping trips. So I found myself looking at old hippy vans. The inner hippy in me was never hidden very deeply. Which is what brought me to an ad for an old VW camper van. It looked good. It looked like me. It was affordable.

I sent the link to my good friend Alex, or Beetle, as I called him. A real hippy, he'd lived in all sorts of vehicles in his time so could give me good advice. He said if it was as sound as it looked from the photos, he would buy it himself had he been in the market for one.

It was over in Issoire, about an hour and a half's drive from the grottage, especially on wintry roads. I enlisted Patrick's help to act as chauffeur and advisor and arranged that he would drive me over and if it was any good, I would drive it back. I took the cash with me, in case.

Rule No 1. If something seems to be too good to be true, it usually is. The first indicator that all was not well was when we arrived at Issoire to find the seller of the VW head-first down inside the engine compartment tinkering away. Despite his best efforts, there was no way the engine was about to spring into life any time soon.

The rust patches around the underside of the bodywork didn't worry me unduly since they seemed to be about the only thing holding it all together. Inside, it boasted its own air conditioning in that there appeared to be draughts coming from cracks that were not even visible to the naked eye. And if there was no shower cubicle, that didn't matter as the roof clearly leaked so abundantly it would be possible to take a shower just by standing in the centre of the living area.

The tyres looked decidedly perished round the sides and were not winter tyres, so even if, which was looking very unlikely, the engine ever started, there was no way it would make it up to the grottage with lying snow on the roads as there was. A quick phone call to my nearest tyre place revealed that the size was now obsolete so it would mean buying new wheel rims to accommodate the nearest available size of tyre, which would very nearly double the cost of buying the van.

Oh well, it was a nice dream whilst it lasted but it seemed as if I was going to have to find something more sensible and practical, and find something soon.

I'd already had a scary moment trying to bump start on icy snow. I'd had to leave Blue with no wheels in contact the road, to avoid it being hit by passing vehicles. This meant I had to push it a few feet to get onto the tarmac. I could usually manage to do so by myself, but with the added problems of frozen solid rutted tyre tracks to get over, I simply couldn't do it.

Luckily, who should be driving past but the Bowing Farmer, whose name I had still not discovered. I flagged him down, explained the problem, and he kindly gave Blue a shove so I reached the road. I then set off rolling merrily along on the Augerolles road, having decided the steep slope down into the hamlet would be too dangerous in the road conditions.

Blue failed to start on the first bump. Or the second. Or the third. So by this time I was getting perilously close to the nasty bend with all the black ice and it would be foolish to attempt to negotiate that without the assistance of engine braking. I simply had to stop, as far to the side of the narrow road as I could, and phone my local garage for breakdown assistance. Because I was not the only one with problems, given the weather, they were not going to be able to attend for at least two hours.

With my 'Be Prepared' nature, I had not only the

obligatory warning triangle and fluorescent vest in the van but also a spare second triangle so I could at least put clear warnings in front and behind. But it was a very dangerous place to be stopped on such bad roads and clearly I couldn't continue to take the risk of further breakdowns. Blue was going to have to go to the big garage in the sky and I was going to have to find something else, urgently.

Almost in passing, as we drove back from our fruitless trip to Issoire, Patrick suggested we call into the Renault garage he used in Courpiere to see if they knew of anything. It was a very small place, they had a few vehicles for sale but, as he said, they also knew others who might have something.

They didn't, as it happened, have anything within my budget, but they did know a man who might. They made a quick phone call to a dealer in nearby Thiers and told me he had a former *La Poste* van with very low mileage, less than fifty thousand kilometres, despite it being seven years old, and in seemingly good condition.

Patrick kindly agreed to drive me straight up there, as things were getting desperate. It was a little over the budget I had set myself, but with such low mileage, it was certainly worth a look.

It wasn't far, so we whizzed up to Thiers and found the car sales place easily enough. Outside was a bright yellow Renault Kangoo van which still had the faint traces of the *La Poste* decals on the sides, where the sun had faded the colour around them.

We went to find the car salesman. From his complexion and slight tremor, I thought he probably enjoyed his drink a little too much. He was altogether so seedy looking, and with such bad breath, he was like a caricature of a second-hand car dealer from an awful sit-com.

He got the keys to show us round the vehicle and clearly thought it a little unusual that I wanted to stretch out on the floor in the back to see if there would be enough room for me to sleep there whilst wild camping. Goodness knows what he thought I was going to be getting up to in it!

Patrick and I then took it for a short spin. It handled quite well and performed everything I asked of it. It was in reasonable condition and as far as we could tell, the low mileage was probably genuine. As a former *La Poste* vehicle, it should, at least, have been regularly serviced and reasonably well looked after.

We braved the confined space of the salesman's cramped office, where his dragon breath was in even greater evidence. He assured us the van would be fully serviced and put through its *controle technique*, the French equivalent of the MOT test in the UK, although one which lasts for two years rather than one. He would, he said, have it ready for me to collect within two days, and would also see to the change of ownership documents.

It seemed like a reasonable vehicle, and the best deal I was likely to get whilst I was in a hurry and therefore vulnerable. I accepted and paid a deposit. Strangely, Mr Dragon Breath didn't want the cash I still had in my bag from the failed earlier transaction, he insisted on a cheque, so I wrote one out for him.

A couple of days later, Patrick drove me back and dropped me off, having first checked that the van was ready. In the office, trying to breathe through vestigial gills to avoid the wafts of halitosis, I paid the balance and collected up the various documents, the *carte grise* or registration document, the *controle technique* certificate, receipt and so on. The CT certificate was totally clean, not even any advisory work to be carried out before the next test, which was reassuring.

France has a clever but simple scheme that makes it a bit harder to drive round in an illegal vehicle. A little sticker for both insurance and *controle technique* must be displayed on the windscreen at all times. My CT sticker was there, and I'd managed to sort out insurance for my new vehicle, so was able to add that.

The van didn't have winter tyres on so I had arranged to stop at my local tyre depot on the way back to change them, as without, it was not possible to drive safely up to the grottage. It was probably overkill but I tended to put winter tyres all round, rather just on the drive wheels, hoping it would afford me a little extra traction when the roads were bad.

I pulled up into the wheel changing bay, shook hands, or rather sleeve cuffs, with the mechanic, that being the normal form of greeting for anyone with dirty hands. He started taking off the front wheels, then the head-shaking and the *'putains'* began.

Rule No 1, remember? If something seems too good to be true, it probably is. According to the mechanic, not only were the front tyres which were on the van illegal in terms of inadequate tread, they were not even a matching pair, so were highly dangerous.

All of which begged the question as to how the van could possibly have been given a totally clean bill of health in its *controle technique* without any comment at all being made about the tyres.

I got the mechanic to give me the illegal tyres and to mark in chalk which wheels they had come off. The rear wheels still had a bit of tread left and were at least a matching pair, so I kept those.

As soon as I got back home, which was easily accomplished with the new tyres making light of the snowy, icy conditions, I phoned Mr Dragon Breath and told him, in no uncertain terms, exactly what I thought of him.

I pointed out that as the van had allegedly been through a *control technique* without the illegal tyres being picked up, it gave me no faith at all in the veracity of the certificate. I said I would be coming back to see him and wanted a new pair of tyres to replace the front ones, and a categorical assurance that the CT had in fact been carried out. I also told him that any subsequent defects found as a result of the test not having been carried out correctly would be down to him to put right at his expense.

In addition, I told him that I would be taking the van to my local *gendarmerie* to inform them of the situation and myself of my legal rights and duties with regard to the bogus certificate. I could almost hear him trembling at the end of the phone line.

The idea of going to the police was not necessarily to take action against Mr Dragon Breath but just to find out exactly where I stood, especially if there was a chance that the vehicle I was now driving round in was not in fact roadworthy at all.

I called at the *gendarmerie* in Olliergues, explained what had happened and an officer came out with me to look at the tyres for himself. He asked where I had bought the van, but I said at that stage, I didn't want to say, I was looking for advice not action. He could, of course, see for himself as the car dealer had put his sticker in the back windscreen, but he made no comment on that. He looked at the mismatched pair of tyres I showed him and said, in no uncertain terms: "Whoever sold you this vehicle with those tyres on was probably an idiot or a crook."

Clearly French policemen don't hold back on their opinions.

He asked me if I wanted to make a formal complaint. I said I would be prepared to give the man a chance to put things rights but that if he refused, I would be straight back ready to throw the book at him.

When I arrived at the car sales showroom, Mr Dragon Breath's slight tremor now resembled that of a gundog which had just heard the unmistakeable sound of a shotgun being cocked. He was positively squirming as he hastened to assure me that nothing like this had ever happened before.

He told me that a mechanic at the test centre had given him the paperwork saying the test had been carried out but had since been dismissed for failing to notice the tyres. He assured me he had had the vehicle serviced and checked before selling it to me, which begged the question how his own mechanic had failed to spot the tyres.

But I needed a vehicle and now it had on the correct tyres, Roo the Kangoo, as I had named the little yellow van, seemed to go well and did at least start on the first turn of the key every time.

I took the brand new tyres he was offering and reminded him once more that, setting aside the three month warranty, anything at all that went wrong in the near future with the van which should reasonably have been picked up on the test would be down to him. I told him what the police had had to say about him but said that on the understanding that he would put things right if problems arose, we could leave it there.

It was with a badly shaking hand he shook mine in agreement. If he had perhaps thought a single English woman would be a pushover, he had just had a rude awakening.

Chapter Ten
Then There Were Two

As a way of improving my French, I tried to listen to French radio as often as possible. I'd discovered France Bleu Pays d'Auvergne, the regional channel, whilst at the physiotherapist, or as I always called them, the physioterrorist, having my dodgy neck realigned yet again.

It was an easy listening channel with popular music, including a lot of English and American singers amongst the French, and some quizzes, which I found both interesting and informative. In the mornings there was a general knowledge quiz, against the clock, and I was always pleased if I could get a few questions right. At lunch time there was a challenge, *Les defis du professeur Gersal,* based on either history and heritage of various French regions, or on French spelling and correct use of words.

Theoretically there is a limit on how much non-French language music the French channels can broadcast, the Toubon Law, so I was also learning more about French singers amongst the English language stuff. I quite liked a lot of the French singers and songs, both the old traditionals like Serge Gainsbourg, and the new generation like Zaz and Nolwenn Leroy.

It's famously difficult to catch the lyrics of a song in any language. There can't be anyone from the Queen generation who doesn't remember the famous misheard lyric of 'Spare him his life for his pork sausages' in Bohemian Rhapsody. For the non-Queen initiated, the words are actually: 'Spare him his life from this monstrosity'.

My own personal best was probably from Dido's 'White Flag'. I did think 'I will go down with this ship, I won't poke my eyes out and surrender' sounded a bit drastic. I was reassured when a Google search revealed the actual lyric as 'I won't put my hands up and surrender'.

So it was not surprising I made similar errors with unfamiliar French lyrics. I thought it was very touching that a vibrant young pop group like Circus should sing about '*chaque mamie*', every granny. In fact it turned out the words are '*chagrin d'ami*', a friend's grief.

One song I really liked was called '*Fais-moi une fleur*' and I would join in enthusiastically, once I'd checked on Google and found the refrain was actually about the song of wisteria plants (*glycines*) not of carbohydrates (*glucides*).

If you've read the earlier books '*Sell the Pig*' and '*Is That Billinge Lump?*' you will know that I love mind games like word association and six degrees of separation. So keep the word *fleur* (flower) in your head as you read on.

For some time I'd been considering getting a second dog. Despite all my best efforts with him, Ci was still nervous and mistrustful of strangers, especially men. He didn't bite, but he would nip if he found himself cornered or felt under threat.

He could be such a gentle and loving dog with me, and always had been with my mother. But in a situation where he felt under pressure, or didn't quite understand what he was supposed to do, he would go rigid, his ears would be plastered to his skull and he would start a low rumbling growl. His tail would disappear from sight between his legs and his eyes would show the classic white-rimming of a seriously worried dog, known as whale eye.

Anything could trigger off the reaction. Asking him to get into the van, which he usually loved, or to come in from the garden sometimes, for reasons known only to him. If I tried to make him obey, the growling would change to bare-toothed snarling, and if I was stupid enough to force the issue, there would be some too-close-for-comfort threat snapping towards my ankles.

I'd long wondered if the presence of a friendly, confident dog would make him better or worse. Our time at a dog club when we lived at the Pink House had been disastrous. It was very regimented, lots of choke chains, lots of shouted commands and no allowances made for a nervous little dog like Ci whose faith in humankind had been shattered by being taken to the refuge and given up for adoption.

France was a bit behind the UK in the emergence of animal behaviourists rather than just trainers, people who would look at the reasons behind a dog's behaviour and work on them, rather than just force compliance. I'd been to consult one but had decided that although he talked the talk, he didn't really walk the walk. More to the point, he was clearly afraid of little Ci and said that as he was an adult dog, there was not much to be done about his behaviour.

My next door neighbour had a little Jack Russell terrier, Étoile, (Star) and she, too had been to see the so-called Dog Whisperer and found him lacking. She mentioned she'd recently seen something in the local paper about a new dog behaviourist, a woman, at a place called Fournols, up in the Haut-Livradois area, about an hour away from the grottage.

I found her contact details online and phoned to make an appointment for a consultation with Ci, up at her training ground in Fournols. It turned out to be a large field literally in the middle of a forest. Caro, as the trainer was called, was already waiting punctually at the gate, but the weather was absolutely awful, pouring down and blowing a hooley. She looked absolutely my type, youngish, no nonsense, no hype, a little touch of the hippy, and clearly knew her stuff.

She suggested we drive into the nearby village for a coffee

and a discussion of Ci's problems in the warmth whilst we waited to see if the weather would improve. As we did so, I explained everything about Ci, including my less than successful experience with the other trainer.

After our coffees, the weather brightened up so we went out to the van. I warned Caro that Ci's normal reaction to anyone he didn't know was to rush at them barking murderously. As I got him out of the van, she squatted right down on her haunches and let him approach her.

Within moments she was wearing my savage, beyond all hope, difficult dog like a scarf and being licked to death. It was a pivotal moment. We joined her weekly class sessions and within in a very short time Ci was politely approaching strangers to introduce himself and even allowing himself to be led away from me by a young girl, with Caro to supervise, when we did swapping dog recalls.

Before I'd had Ci, I'd dreamed of getting a female dog, with a golden coat. I'd had a succession of black and white dogs, Ci being my fifth collie, so I fancied a colour change. I started keeping an eye on the website of the refuge near Clermont-Ferrand where I had found and adopted Ci.

And then one day, I couldn't believe my eyes. There on the page was a beautiful sable and white border collie, just eighteen months old, and in the refuge for the second time in her short life. She had the most amazing Bollywood eyes which looked as if they had been highlighted with Kohl pencil. According to the blurb, Fleur, as she was called, was friendly and loved everyone.

There had to be a Rule No 1 clause, but at least I had to go and see for myself. Unfortunately it was a Monday evening and I knew the refuge was closed to visitors and adoptions on Tuesdays, so I would have to wait.

I was on pins all day as I couldn't believe such a lovely looking dog would stay there very long before being snapped up, especially as border collies were currently the most popular breed in France.

So the next morning, Ci and I were up early and arrived outside the refuge, before the gates were even open. Ci was very agitated, as he knew exactly where he was and was clearly very worried that he might be going to be left there again.

Several of the volunteers who go to walk the dogs and help clean them out were gathering outside the gate so I took the opportunity to chat to them about Fleur. They all knew her and said she was lovely and they thought she was still there and still available for adoption. Some of them remembered Ci from his time there.

As soon as the gates were open, I went straight to the reception desk to see if Fleur was still available. She was. Could I please see her?

Even though I'd been before, my ears were scarcely prepared for the cacophony of barking, howling and yelping that assailed them the minute I walked through the building and into the yard outside where the kennels were. The refuge was always full to overflowing, and as usual, dogs were crammed two and three into a pen so the noise was almost unbearable.

A young man led me over to a pen and there was Fleur. Every bit as blonde and beautiful as she looked on the website, and all licky and wiggly and giggly with pleasure at having people to talk to her. She was sharing the pen with a big setter and didn't seem to have any problem with his presence, which was a good sign.

She was let out of the pen and came and wiggled and squiggled all over me, with much licking and cuddling. She really was gorgeous to look at, and her story was a sad one. She had been found straying at just under a year old, not micro-chipped or identified in any way and never claimed. She was chipped and spayed by the refuge then re-homed with a young couple who subsequently decided to split up. Sadly neither could, or would, accept responsibility for Fleur so she was sent back to the refuge.

I explained about Ci and how nervous he was with other dogs and said there was probably not a lot of point in introducing them at the refuge as he would be so stressed by the location, he would not be at all relaxed. But the man suggested we try a short walk together, him leading Fleur and me with Ci, just to see what their initial reaction was.

It must be a desperately difficult job to work in a place like a refuge. Even the best and the most humanely run of them have an air of 'abandon hope all ye who enter here' about them. I noticed that the young man was quite rough in his handling of the dogs, the way he shoved the setter back into the pen, and grabbed a couple of escapees that came rushing past us. I suppose a certain hardening was a way of getting through a difficult occupation.

Ci may have remembered him, or was maybe just being his usual man-hating self, but he certainly barked aggressively at the sight of him. Fleur bounced over to Ci quite unafraid and tried her best to make friends but he was a bit too preoccupied. He didn't show any open aggression, though, which was a positive sign.

In an ideal world, any adoption from a refuge is preceded by a thorough home inspection. But the world of unwanted dogs is far from ideal and this refuge was just so overwhelmed with numbers they were delighted to be able to offload inmates to anyone remotely suitable.

I had been given Ci as I'd gone with someone I knew, Hippy Chick, one of my mother's former carers, who had vouched for me. All I'd had to do was provide a utility bill as proof of residence. And he'd hardly been a gift; the cost of adopting a dog was €240, although that did include chipping, neutering and vaccination.

On the documents, Fleur was down as a border collie cross and marked as a tricolour. She looked absolutely pure border to me, and I'd had a few, but the French didn't seem to know the sable and white as a border collie colour.

The standard procedure was to take the dog on a week's trial to see if the match was suitably mutually satisfactory. As I'd already had one dog from them, there was no problem at all in taking Fleur on trial. I paid the deposit cheque, signed all the forms, and headed to the van with my potentially new dog.

I'd put the big travel cage in the back of the van to keep the dogs separate on the journey back, to make for a safer drive home with me alone in the van with the two of them. I put Ci into the cage and left Fleur loose in the back of the van behind it.

In typical collie fashion, Fleur liked to zoom to and fro at the sight of other traffic, and did little yip noises a bit like an excitable chimpanzee. But generally she behaved quite well and showed no signs of being travel sick.

There was still no sign of any aggression between the two dogs so once we got back to the grottage, I took them both into the enclosed garden, let them off their leads and let them get on with it.

Ci was a bit clueless about interaction with other dogs. He didn't seem to have had much socialisation before I had him and was always nervous. Fleur was just an out and out flirt. She would rush up to him, play bow, wag her tail and smile, then whiz off at high speed and do several laps of the garden before he could work out what was going on.

Eventually he got the idea of chasing after her and finally, seemed to be discovering that dog play was actually really good fun. Before long they both plonked down panting, clearly quite happy in each other's company.

My dogs always sleep with me. In my bedroom, on the bed, if they chose, but I like them as close as possible. If a burglar should break into my house, I want the dogs to protect me, not the silver.

Ci usually prefers to sleep underneath the bed rather than on it and, not yet knowing Fleur's preference, I had put down a fleecy blanket in a corner of the room where she might feel secure. I showed her where she could sleep. She seemed to know the basic commands already, so I got her to lie down on the blanket whilst I got ready for bed.

As soon as she saw me settling into my lovely bed, with its expensive, custom-made mattress, she was across the bedroom with the speed of a ferret up a drainpipe and up onto the bed beside me. She gave me a very knowing look as she curled herself into a neat ball, her tail over her nose like a little fox, and snuggled comfortably into the small of my back.

That was one little dog who was certainly not going back to the refuge at the end of the week's trial.

Chapter Eleven
Kevin the Kitchen Range

The winters in my new home were certainly going to be challenging. It was at almost exactly the same altitude as the Pink House but in a region which tended to get quite a bit more snow and it often felt much colder there.

I was going to need some form of relatively inexpensive heating to keep my little grottage warm. Alf and Bert, the vendors, had put on a new roof before selling it, covering up the existing tiny chimney conduit. Their reasoning was that there was mains gas available quite close to, and they thought the new owner might like to connect to that and have everything clean, modern and running on gas.

My preference was for something much more traditional for all sorts of reasons, especially eco ones. There was plenty of good, sustainable hardwood growing in the area, available at a reasonable cost. I wanted some sort of wood-burning range in the kitchen on which to cook in the cooler weather. The right one would hopefully heat most of the grottage, which was only small and reasonably well insulated, with good double glazing in the newly-installed windows.

Because it was a back to back semi-detached house, with the other half of the building to the north side, it was fairly well protected from the worst of the weather, which would help to reduce heating bills to a degree.

Trawling the various advertising sites and local papers for a second hand kitchen range which would fit the bill was a bit depressing. Yet another thing which tended to be pricier here in rural France than in the UK.

The semi-retired builder from round the corner had made me a smart new exterior chimney. Because of trying to fit in between roof trusses, it wasn't in exactly the ideal place for the straightforward connection of a kitchen range. With a little ingenuity, it should be doable, just about.

One day, Patrick asked me if I would like a dog kennel for Ci, this being shortly before Fleur had joined the family. He explained he had made it for his family dog which, being a real roughy-toughy type of farm dog, far preferred to sleep outside on a concrete slab than in anything as poncey as a wooden kennel.

Knowing how well Patrick made things, I knew it would be substantial and said I would be delighted to have it for Ci. I added that I couldn't possibly accept it as a gift, I would have to give him something, at least, towards its cost.

He said I should take a look at it and invited me up for an evening meal. Almost in passing, he said he had an old kitchen range he wanted to get rid of, having bought it for his own house then never installed it.

Eating with Patrick and his family was always enjoyable. His wife, Cecilia, was one of the most spontaneously funny and vivacious people I have met. She spoke incredibly quickly and taxed my French to its limits. She had an extremely broad interest in anything and everything and whatever the topic of discussion was, she would inject humour into the conversation so that my cheeks would soon be aching from smiling and laughing.

The first time I visited their home, I discovered an interesting thing about Patrick. He was a total geography buff. He asked me what part of England I came from. I explained that I was born in Cheshire but had been living in Lincolnshire before moving to France. Since many English people don't know where Lincolnshire is, I added a rough explanation.

'Is that near Kingston upon Hull?' he asked, causing me almost to fall off my seat in amazement. Again many English people would struggle to locate Hull on a map, let alone give it its correct full title. And he was right, it was close, just over the Humber estuary from North Lincolnshire.

He brought out a map from his large collection and spread it on the big refectory type dining table, asking me whereabouts in Lincolnshire I had lived.

Since the hamlet I'd lived in, Stanton le Vale, boasted fewer than two dozen houses and a church, I mentioned it in passing but said it was situated about halfway between the county seat of Lincoln, and the town of Grimsby, on the coast.

But Patrick's was a geography buff's map. It actually had tiny Stanton le Vale on it, much to my surprise. It was not just UK geography Patrick knew intimately. His world geography in general was impressive. I discovered brains very much ran in his family when I met his brother one time. He was visiting the area to take part in a national Mastermind type of quiz in which he was currently lying in eleventh position of two hundred and fifty contestants.

At one point I arranged with the son and daughter-in-law of a friend of mine that Patrick's teenage daughter should go and stay with them in England for three weeks to help improve her English. Julie was a talented singer-songwriter who often wrote songs in English but recognised she had some work to do on her accent.

The young couple who would be her hosts lived in Somerset and Patrick didn't even need to consult the maps to know that Southampton would be the nearest airport for a flight from Clermont-Ferrand. Although like many French people, he struggled to pronounce the Th, especially in the middle of a word.

That became an in joke between us. There's a town not far from the grottage which is called Cunlhat – not a typing error!

Most of the locals pronounce it as something like Cuh-ya, or sometimes Cye to rhyme with eye and a, the short sound, as at the start of apple. Kye-ya. But I've heard so many variations on the pronunciation of it that when I talk to Patrick about the place, I always call it Southampton.

The dog kennel, as I suspected, was a robust and well made piece of kit. It was certainly a good size for Ci as Cookie, the dog for whom it was built, was bigger and more solid. He just didn't fancy it. Patrick had told me his dog was some sort of collie cross. As soon as I saw him, I was able to tell him he was, in fact, rather a nice sable and white Australian shepherd dog.

Inside the barn adjoining Patrick's house was a white wood-burning kitchen range of the French make Rosières .It looked the right sort of thing and I knew the brand was fairly reliable. I asked about price. Patrick named a figure, Cecilia immediately said it was too high and reduced it.

I pointed out it was customary for the purchaser to haggle the price down, rather than the vendors. We arrived at a price which seemed reasonable to me, with the dog kennel thrown in as a freebie. Patrick said he would arrange some reinforcements to transport the range up to the grottage, as it was ferociously heavy, and he would then install it.

Trying to construct a flue which would link up easily from where the range had to be put, to where the exterior chimney was situated was not at all easy. It finished up with a couple of bends, which was not ideal. But once the range was lit, it was soon roaring away and looked like a success.

It soon transpired that I had not so much bought a kitchen range as a spotty teenager with attitude. Some days the range worked marvellously, warming the grottage and enabling me to cook a full meal. Other days, for no reason discernible to me, it would sulk and smoke and burn with all the warmth of two candle-power.

A Facebook friend of mine, Fiona, reminded me of the two

rebellious teenagers in the Harry Enfield television sketches, Kevin and Perry. From then on, the range became known as Kevin the Kitchen Range and seemed to take on a personality all of its own.

My work station was in the kitchen, which was warmer and roomier than the sitting room, so I sat with my back to Kevin, and my computer screen almost directly opposite him.

He could be burning away merrily and I would just mention on social media that I was about to cook my supper. In the time it took me to get pans and ingredients out and ready, Kevin would be reduced to a small glowing ember at the end of one log and nothing much else.

Fortunately, my motto has always been: 'I like a challenge', so I soldiered on, alternately coaxing, cajoling and cursing Kevin into performing. He continued to alternate his performance between one which would put a blast furnace to shame and an output slightly lower than a cheap tea light out of a bag of one hundred from the pound shop.

Of course, he was always at his hottest on the mildest evenings and his coldest when I wanted to bake something. I'm not a bad baker, I can usually turn out something decent, given the right oven temperature. Cakes were a disaster with Kevin, though. He would either refuse to heat up, so they just melted all over his oven like volcanic lava, or he roared away too viciously, giving them a burnt and blackened top and a runny, soggy middle.

I desperately needed to keep Kevin on side as the kitchen had to stay warm overnight to stop the water from freezing up. The entry point for the mains water was underneath where the sink had been before I got Patrick to move it under the window, to take advantage of the view and the light. It was now in a curtained off shelved area where I kept the pans.

It can get very cold here, down to almost minus twenty Celsius in the night. The water pipes ran against the front wall of the house and were prone to freezing up, especially when the wind was in the wrong direction.

On a couple of mornings I had woken to find the water frozen and had to do some ungainly scrambling about amongst the pans with a little folding travel hair dryer to gently restore the flow. If Kevin agreed to stay in through the night, it kept the temperature up sufficiently, even in that cold corner, to stop them freezing.

But in typical teenager fashion, when I wanted Kevin to stay in, he went out and when I would have been quite happy for him to go out, he chose to stay in.

Patrick had several goes at re-configuring Kevin's flue pipes to try to get him to behave, but he continued to follow his own agenda, blazing away magnificently when it was warm outside, sulking and refusing to go at all, or going out, when it was cold.

Teenagers, eh? Got to love them!

Chapter Twelve
The Bitey Snake

Life was looking good. The little grottage was reasonably snug and cosy and certainly liveable in, by my modest standards. There was still a lot of finishing off to do, but between my best BIY efforts, and Patrick still doing bits when he had time, I was pleased with how it had all come together.

It was doubtful if the project would ever be completely finished in my lifetime. I lacked the funds to do much more. Certainly converting the barn into an airy work studio, then adding a bedroom, as I hankered to do, was way beyond my resources, unless I had a big win on the premium bonds. But it was all fine for the time being, more than fine, in fact. The views were so beautiful, and I spent so much time outdoors, I barely had time to notice little details like the odd door not yet stripped down and varnished..

Rule No 1, remember? There had to be a 'but'. In this case, it was my health. I'd had periods of feeling really sickly and not wanting to eat off and on for months now, certainly more than a year. It wasn't connected to anything specific which I could identify but it was increasingly affecting me and I had lost a bit of weight.

I was incredibly tired, too. Some nights I would sleep for up to eleven hours. Fortunately, despite being a real live-wire and full of energy, once Fleur was snuggled up on the bed with me, she was happy to sleep as long as I was. Ci could also manage long nights, as long as he was not battling one of the bouts of cystitis he got because of his wonky-shaped bladder.

When I was first exploring the area with Ci, before we got Fleur, I would buy maps and guide books of all the walks around and about and go off and explore them. I've always loved walking, but increasingly was struggling to walk six kilometres and some days, it was as much as I could manage to walk one. Sometimes I just felt like curling up in a ball at the side of the footpath and sleeping for a while. Fortunately, Ci wouldn't hear of it.

Time to visit my new GP and see if she was as good as everyone said and also to find out if the waiting time was as bad as Patrick had claimed.

The doctor was slim, dynamic, probably in her forties, and very thorough. As usual, I didn't even enquire if she spoke English; we spoke in French. She checked my blood pressure, my heart and lungs. Did I know I had a heart murmur? No, I didn't, but I had been told I'd had one as a baby, whilst battling the whooping cough which very nearly carried me off.

She ordered up a huge list of blood tests and said she would see what that produced, as for the moment, she could not immediately identify any possible cause.

Nor did the blood tests, particularly. A couple of things were just outside the normal range, notably ferritin and calcium, but there was no sudden light bulb moment which enabled the doctor to exclaim a delighted 'Eureka!' and tell me exactly what was wrong with me. Her next move was to refer me to a consultant gastroenterologist.

Despite living out in the sticks, I was well served for medical facilities to choose from, and in France it was at that time a matter of choice, too. You were free to pick which hospital to go to for such referrals, no question of being told which one, except for some procedures requiring special equipment which may not be available everywhere.

Both Thiers and Ambert, each within half an hour's drive

of the grottage, boasted a reasonable small hospital and if I was brave enough to tackle the city traffic, Clermont-Ferrand had a large and very good university hospital. Good medically speaking, although its finances were in a slightly worse state than my own.

Based on nothing more scientific than the road being less twisty than the Ambert one, and my in-built hatred of driving to any city, even one as relatively small as Clermont-Ferrand, I chose the Thiers hospital and phoned for an appointment.

I had to wait four weeks, which was quite long for normal French waiting times, but it seemed gastroenterologists were busy people. Mine was also late for our appointment, though not very much so.

He was small and slight and looked quite young to be a consultant. He listened to my symptoms, looked at the various blood results and the letter from my doctor and said he would like to do a *gastroscopie,* a camera passed down the throat, to find out what was going on inside my digestive tract.

Oh joy! I had already had one of those when I lived in Lincolnshire and was having some digestive problems and I did not enjoy it, not at all. I told the consultant this and he assured me that in the intervening twelve or so years, the technology had improved. The camera, on its long flexible probe, was now much smaller, causing less discomfort, and the procedure could be carried out very quickly. A slot was booked for me a fortnight later.

My kind friend Christine volunteered to come and drive me there to make sure I was all right. She was a former midwife so knew about medical matters, though not particularly that end! It would be nice to have some company, especially as, having already had the procedure once before, I knew it was unpleasant so I was bound to be tense.

We left in plenty of time for the appointment as I am a bit of a punctuality freak. Also, one of the problems of the roads round here is not just the frequent encounters with tractors and slow-moving agricultural machinery but also the dreaded *voitures sans permis,* micro-cars, which in France require no driving licence.

Legally classified as motorised quadricycles, they are restricted to a top speed of 45mph which many of them can only achieve going down a very steep hill with a substantial tail wind.

Younger drivers now need a moped licence to drive them, but it does mean they can be on the road earlier than having to wait for their full car licence. But for older people, they require neither driving licence nor any form of medical examination to drive them. So you can form your own opinion of the type of people who might be out and about behind the wheel of these little contraptions, which boast all the performance of a sewing machine.

Presumably to target the younger market, they now come in a variety of body styles, including a coupé, and with added finishing touches like metallic paint. Get stuck behind them on a stretch of road where there is no overtaking, and they might as well be a ride-on mower.

We didn't encounter any, so we were at the hospital in plenty of time. Christine escorted me up to the unit I'd been told to report to, to stop me doing a runner on the way, saw me settled then went off to get herself a drink and a sandwich and sit in the sunshine with her book. How I envied her!

I was told to change into an open-backed hospital gown, disposable slippers and a very fetching paper hat, then await collection. Someone came with a wheelchair and wheeled me to the lift and from there, down seemingly into the bowels of the hospital and into a tiny holding room where I was transferred to a trolley and my glasses were taken away.

Although I can see shapes well enough without glasses, everything is very blurred and being minus my specs tends to make me feel a bit vulnerable. I also find it harder to hear and understand people, especially when they speak French to me, as I pick up a lot of visual clues like facial expressions to grasp meaning and nuance.

From there I was pushed, on the trolley, into a corridor and deposited, presumably to await the arrival of the consultant. Several nurses passed me, all greeting me with a friendly '*Bonjour*' as they passed, some stopping to check the notes on the trolley with me, to see if I was one of theirs.

Many of them wore long gowns, down to ankle length and had their heads covered, but with my blurred vision I couldn't tell if this was standard hospital wear or cultural attire.

After a while I was wheeled into an adjacent room with big high windows, which looked rather like the science laboratories at my secondary school. The nurses who were in there said the consultant was running late because he had to come from another clinic where he consulted, in Vichy. They apologised for the delay and started chatting to me to help the time pass.

There was something of an air of tension about them that was doing nothing to ease my anxiety, which was increasing with every moment's delay. And once the dapper little consultant finally swept into the room, the tension was ratcheted up another few notches immediately. I hoped it was because he was something of a martinet, although I felt sorry for the nurses if he was. As long as it wasn't because of his patient mortality rate.

As soon as he arrived, one of the nurses sprayed the back of my throat with a bitter-tasting substance which was meant to numb the area slightly to minimise discomfort. Then a type of gag was inserted into my mouth to hold it open and to stop me from biting down on the valuable camera.

The consultant then started to pass the flexible tube down my throat and I had to swallow to see it on its way. That was the point at which I realised French consultants lie. It was every bit as big and uncomfortable as the last one I had swallowed.

My gag reflex is very overdeveloped. I even heave if my toothbrush touches the back of my tongue whilst I'm cleaning my teeth. At this point my stomach was starting to buck and retch in protest.

The nurses leaned over me and said, not unkindly: *'Calmez-vous, madame, respirez.'* , 'calm down, madam, breathe.' Easy for you to say, you haven't just swallowed a live anaconda which is busily wriggling its way round your insides.

The hardest part was not being allowed to swallow once the camera had started to go down. I was told not to swallow, just to allow any saliva to drain out of my open mouth. But of course, not only did that feel very unpleasant but it's quite a common reaction to want to do exactly the thing one has been told not to do.

Luckily, true to his word this time, the consultant was in and out fairly quickly, so the ordeal did not last very long. The worst part, as on the previous occasion, was when he pulled the camera out as it felt like my intestines were coming with it. But at least it was then over and the consultant did tell me immediately that he had not found anything sinister. He said there was some chronic gastritis and that he would write to my doctor to discuss that, but there was nothing else to see at the moment.

Back up on the unit, I could get changed into my own clothes. I was offered a drink and something to eat but all I really wanted to do was get out and go home. From the window of the cubicle in which I got changed, I was able to look down to the car park and see Christine sitting reading in the sunshine.

What I wanted most of all was a massive cup of tea, a large sticky bun, since I'd had nothing to eat since the previous evening, and a hug from my dogs. Christine drove me back, stopping on the way in the nearby town of Courpiere to call in at the *boulangerie* for delicious cakes.

Back at the grottage, we made mugs of tea and sat outside

the front door in the sunshine with them and our cakes. I still didn't know exactly what was wrong with me but at least nothing too alarming had shown up so far.

Chapter Thirteen
Year's Mind

Time was flying by. It was already a year since my mother had died. Anniversaries can be difficult, especially when they coincide with birthdays. Apparently it is statistically very common for people to die on their birthday – Shakespeare did. My father died the evening before his and my mother died just days after hers.

I decided a change of scene and a change of air might be in order to mark the occasion. I'm not much of a seaside person, but Mother loved collecting sea-shells and pretty pebbles from the beach, so I thought a couple of days of sea air would be fitting. Perhaps it might also help shake off whatever nagging health problem was making me feel like a sickly zombie much of the time.

Living in the Massif Central, it was a long drive west or south in search of the sea. I mentally dismissed the south coast, worried there would be too many people about. A Facebook friend, Victoria, kindly told me about a place on the south-western coast of Aquitaine called Le Porge Océan, which boasted thirteen kilometres of beach. She said it tended to be quiet in spring, which sounded perfect for me.

Roo the Kangoo had been behaving very well since I bought it, and this would be the first long run since I'd had it. I estimated that, driving slowly and with frequent stops to water the dogs, it would probably take me about five hours to get to my destination.

My chosen route would take me on my first visit through the Dordogne, or as it was affectionately known, Dordogneshire, because of its high numbers of British ex-pats. The Dordogne boasts one town with a population of more than thirty per cent British incomers. It was the main reason I had never been attracted to it, but it would be nice to see some of its scenery on the way down.

An internet search showed a few camp-sites in the vicinity. Most of them seemed not to open until the first of April and I was going down two days before. The weather was absolutely glorious, warm sunshine and not a sign of a cloud, so I thought perhaps at least one of them would be enterprising enough to open their gates earlier than advertised.

The journey would be quite a testing one as Fleur had decided travelling was so much fun she liked to yip like a demented chimpanzee from the moment I first let off the handbrake to the time we arrived at our destination. Ci, bless him, had always been an excellent traveller, quiet and well behaved. But despite all my best efforts, Fleur was still a bit of a nightmare. I had even resorted to wearing earplugs.

Helpful people offered advice which was not practical. Apart from the fact that I'd worked in therapy so knew about the 'ignore the bad behaviour and reward the wanted behaviour' theory, there was never any good behaviour to reward. She squeaked non-stop. It's a wonder long-suffering Ci didn't just bite her or sit on her.

I'd now been living in my beloved Auvergne for five years and had not once left its boundaries in that time. Nor even wanted to. So this was going to be a bit of an adventure.

I'd decided to use motorways most of the way, simply for the speed and convenience. Once I left the comforting confines of the Auvergne, I crossed first into Limousin, which I had previously visited. I'd spent a few days there wobbling about on a hired bicycle with an exceedingly uncomfortable saddle. It was nice enough, but again, there were too many Brits in evidence for my particular taste.

When I left the Limousin and arrived in the Dordogne, I couldn't believe how many people there were everywhere. The motorway was heaving and when I stopped at a service station, it was almost impossible to find a parking space there were so many vehicles about. I decided the dogs and I would just have to cross our legs for a bit longer and carry on.

Crossing Bordeaux and its heavy traffic was a nightmare. If we had not now been so far from home and so near our destination, I would have been tempted to turn back to the peace and quiet of the Auvergne. But at last we were back onto quiet country roads with the tang of the sea breezes in our nostrils. After such a long and tiring drive, the dogs and I were eager to stretch our legs, and maybe even dip our toes in the Atlantic Ocean, if it wasn't too cold.

Following signs to the beach, I drove past the municipal camp-site at the top of a hill, resolutely closed, despite the glorious weather and the large number of forlorn holiday makers driving around clearly looking for somewhere to spend the night. At the bottom of the hill was a wooded parking area with signs everywhere prohibiting wild camping or parking for motor-homes. At last we were able to park in cool shade and all pile out of the van, stretching stiffness from legs and paws. A short walk through soft sand and welcome duck-boards to make it easier, through a gap in the sand dunes and there before us was the mighty Atlantic Ocean, with golden sand stretching as far as the eye could see in either direction.

Victoria had been right about the lack of people. Even on a sunny afternoon, there were few about and there was so much room there was no need to be on top of one another.

We had a brilliant time. The dogs scampered about like mad things, and even I was tempted by the bracing sea breeze to do a little capering with them. We all dipped our feet in any pools of water left by the outgoing tide and even braved the very shallowest of the waves.

I picked up pretty shells for Mother, pink and peach, and unusual pebbles, shiny ones, marbled ones. The dogs dug enormous holes in the sand, spraying one another and me with great flurries of damp sand. We walked and walked and with so much open space, if anyone approached to encroach on our peace, we could simply turn around and walk in another direction.

Then we headed back to the van and did our best to shake as much sand from ourselves as we could. It was now late afternoon, time to start thinking of where we were going to rest our weary heads for the night. With the nearest camp-site closed and me not wanting to drive any further after the long journey down, I thought I'd just find a quiet spot close to the beach to park up and we could all sleep in the van for the night. As wild camping was not allowed, I wasn't going to get the tent out. I didn't think a little Kangoo van would count as a motorhome so I hoped we wouldn't be breaking any laws.

The parking area was very large, spread out over several wooded acres. First I found a nice quiet spot with a picnic table where I could prepare an evening meal and eat it in peace. The area was incredibly dry after a winter with little precipitation, and the whole woodland was like a tinderbox, so I was even more careful than usual with my little camping stove and the matches I used to light it.

Once I'd eaten and walked the dogs once more, I drove on a little further into the woods onto a small side road with no-one about and prepared to settle down. I got out my camping chair and a book and was reading peacefully when I noticed what appeared to be some sort of forest rangers' vehicle slowly patrolling. It made several passes, never stopping to approach anyone, but the intention was clear. They were checking to see no-one was breaking the 'No wild camping' rules.

Darkness was starting to fall so rather than wait around to be physically escorted from the parking area, I decided I'd better slink away and find another quiet spot in which to park for the night, one which did not have any signs prohibiting wild camping. Theoretically in France, wild camping is allowed anywhere except the national parks, unless there are signs expressly forbidding it.

I headed up the hill to where the camp-site was and found a bit of a lay-by opposite, with an area partly screened from the road by trees and decided to settle down there for the night. As the road only went down to the beach, where parking was clearly not encouraged at night, I knew it would be quiet and I was never afraid of sleeping in the van anywhere. If anyone wanted to brave the wrath of my ferocious guard dogs, they were welcome to try!

We actually passed a very comfortable night and all slept well, no doubt due to the sea breezes. At one point in the night, the dogs and I all got up for a comfort break. A solemn-eyed roe deer was watching us from in the nearby woods. It clearly thought it had seen it all now, an eccentric old hippy woman emerging from the back of a decorated van to go and spend a penny under the moonlight.

Although I hadn't got the hippy van I'd hoped for, I'd decided to give Roo the Kangoo a bit of a hippy makeover. I'd discovered an excellent firm in the UK, Hippy Motors, who sold decals, or, as the French had taken to calling them, *stickers*, although they pronounced them as 'steekairs'. I'd ordered a load, choosing designs that represented a bit about who I am. Local reaction was mixed, from looking at the van as if it was something from outer space, to delight and several requests for Hippy Motors' contact details.

The bonnet was resplendent with a big red dragon, as I was born in a Chinese year of the dragon. One door had the Green Man, to reflect my pagan leanings. The wings were covered in poppies, the only red flower I actually like, to represent one of my favourite poems, by the war poet Isaac Rosenberg, Break of Day in the Trenches.

My personal favourite was the sign on the back door which said: 'Where have all the hippies gone?' Many of the local French might not have been able to understand it, but hippies was a pretty international word, so they got the idea.

In the morning, after a quick cup of tea, we headed back down the hill to the shoreline. I picnicked in the parking area on my favourite *pain au chocolat*, then headed once more over the dunes to the beach. It was absolutely amazing, I counted five whole fishermen on the entire thirteen kilometre stretch.

After another walk and a romp and some more shells collected, I decided I had better go on a mission to find a proper camp-site, as I was planning on staying two more nights. The camp-site I'd parked opposite still showed no signs at all of being open and in fact there were municipal workman doing all sorts of jobs all over the site, so I thought I'd find somewhere a little quieter. First stop was the nearest small town where I found a tourist office to ask.

The lady in the office was very helpful and gave me lots of brochures of the area. She agreed that it was short-sighted of the local communes not to open their sites early to take advantage of all the people descending on the area to enjoy the lovely weather.

Armed with the brochures and her directions, I headed off to find a camp-site. I was careful about which one I picked as I knew there was a big naturist site and beach in the area which, bizarrely, it seemed to me, boasted the world's largest naturist golf course. I wasn't entirely comfortable with the notion of getting my kit off in front of strangers, and certainly averse to the idea of a round of golf in the buff.

The one I arrived at first was large, handily close to some shops for provisions, and within two minutes of pitching my tent, I knew it was not for us. There was just too much traffic noise for it to be peaceful.

Thank goodness for the Quechua two-second tent. It was almost as quick to collapse it and fold it away as it had been to put up, so I could go back to reception, apologise profusely, say it was not for me and ask for a refund. The girl was very kind but said the road was quieter at night. I suspected her definition of quiet was not the same as mine.

I found another site, further inland, from one of the brochures, and having rung to find if they were open, headed there instead. We'd done our bit at the beach and had picked up all the shells and pebbles I thought Mother would have chosen, so now if we were away from the ocean, it wouldn't matter, as long as it was quiet and there were places to walk the dogs.

This time it was a much better site, quieter and much more rural, opening directly onto a forest at the back, which was very handy for walks. Quiet, except that I made the mistake of picking a pitch next to the *boules* court. Or *pétanque*, perhaps, I never understood the difference. So in the evening, large groups of French campers would come down to play, whilst I tried to persuade the dogs not the bark at them.

I had hoped to walk the seven kilometres or so from the camp to the beach the following day but it turned out there was a very impressive dyke between it and the ocean, presumably as a form of flood barrier. But the dogs enjoyed the walk to the dyke and back through the woods.

The forest all around was nice to walk in, long, level sandy tracks and very quiet. It also had the biggest pine cones I'd ever seen. Knowing Mother would have loved those, I collected a big bagful to take back with me as a souvenir.

Then it was time to load the van up once more and head back north-east to the quiet green tranquillity of the Auvergne.

Goodbye ocean, bye-bye Bordeaux, ta-ta Dordogne, *au revoir* Limousin. And soon it was *rebonjour*, hello again, my lovely Auvergne. I won't be leaving your confines again for a long time to come.

Chapter Fourteen
Herding Cats

If you've never seen the television advert about cowboys herding cats, you really should try to find it on YouTube. It's very funny, and perfectly illustrates that cats are a law unto themselves.

My two cats, HRH the Princess Freddie and her loyal lady-in-waiting Bibi, had settled in very well to their new life. They lived in the big barn, where they had at least a dozen cosy boxes and nesting places to choose from. HRH, as befits of princess of royal Siamese descent (only on her father's side, but she behaved as if she was a pure blood) made a point of sleeping in a different one every night – because she could.

I let them out by day, whenever the weather was nice enough, and when there were no drunken men with shotguns and hounds in the next fields. They both came back in before dark every day. If either was running late, they were very good and would come to call.

Bibi liked to go down to the bottom of the field in front of the barn and into the little allotment behind, with its wooden cabin. I suspect there were plenty of mice underneath it. I would sometimes see her sitting on its roof, probably hoping for a bird as a change of menu. When I called her, it was like a scene from 'The Littlest Hobo' or 'Lassie Come Home.' She would come galloping to me, hurdling the fences on the way, and would burst into the hay loft up the long wooden ramp I'd placed there so the cats could get in and out.

Patrick had made me wooden decks for sitting areas. The ground in front of the grottage sloped away, so by making a deck, raised on stout wooden posts, it greatly increased the sitting out area. Since I preferred to be outside as much as possible, it was a real boon.

I'd also got him to make a small raised deck in front of the upper door leading into the hay loft where the cats lived. This was up three wooden steps and had a picket fence all around it, effectively giving the cats a safe air lock so the dogs could not get to them. Both Ci and Fleur liked to chase them. Once they got a bit close to HRH who bloodied Ci's nose for him, so he would now always back off, but Fleur tended to nip when she got excited, which was often.

Neither cat was in the least afraid of the dogs, though, and they seemed to make a sport out of teasing them. They had it timed to a fraction of a second, and their approach was as different as they each were to the other. Bibi liked to go in and out of the cellar's open window, which was situated underneath the deck in front of the house. She'd wait until she knew exactly where the dogs were, then dash out across the open ground in front of the big barn doors and up onto the corner post of the picket fence, with her tail tucked carefully out of reach of dogs' eager jaws.

HRH's style was decidedly eccentric, and quite out of her haughty, regal character. She clearly had a sense of humour! She could come roaring down the garden, sprint up the wooden steps then, instead of simply jumping over the small gate, she would leap in the air, and plant all four feet against the wall at her side, using it as a launch-pad to propel herself onto the deck like a free runner.

I always shut them away at night because there were marauding foxes and pine martens and also herds of feral cats, some quite unpleasant, like the big green-eyed tom, *Feu Vert*, who would attack them at every opportunity. HRH was once slightly late for curfew so spent a very grumpy few hours sitting in Ci's kennel until I came back out and let her into the barn.

Then one evening, there was no sign of HRH at all. I called and called, looked in all her favourite hidey holes, but she wasn't anywhere to be found. I took the dogs out and we scoured the ditches at the sides of all the lanes in case she'd been hit by a car. Still no sign.

All night I kept an ear open for her little bell but neither I nor the dogs heard her, and there was still no sign of her by the next afternoon. I went out on the electric bike so I could look further afield, calling her as I went. Whenever I encountered anyone, I stopped and asked if they had seen a little seal point cat with piercing blue eyes. No-one had seen her, and they all said she would be fine, cats wander off then come back when it suits them, and at this time of year, there was plenty about for a cat to eat, with mice, birds, frogs and even lizards in abundance.

I had never actually seen HRH catch anything. She probably thought that was a servant's job. When she was in her outdoor run at the Pink House, which I called the Winter Palace, I had once found her playing rather absent-mindedly with a venomous aspic viper, but she'd certainly shown no intention of killing it.

After a second night, I was really starting to get worried. It was so out of character for her, and I kept expecting her to pop up at any moment, but there was no sign, and no sound of the little tinkly bell on her pink, sparkly collar.

As the days passed, I grew increasingly anxious with no sightings at all, not even on the distant horizon. I made posters with a photograph and printed them out to pin up around the immediate area. I cycled up to St Loo and St Dongle to put some there.

There was a recycling point near the church for bottles, plastics, paper etc and a lot of people stopped off there on their way past. There was also an ordinary refuse bin, used mainly by people visiting the cemetery and wanting to dispose of old or faded flowers from the graves. I hoped a lot of people would see the poster and perhaps take a look in their outbuildings, in case she had got shut in.

The recycling point was also a magnet for two of the more eccentric near-neighbours. I had often seen a woman driving about in an ancient Renault 5 absolutely stuffed to the gunwales with full black plastic bin-bags, and wondered about her story. There was also an older man in an old and dirty yellow plastic coat, who buzzed about on a little motor scooter, also with bags and boxes attached wherever they would fit on.

My neighbour said they were brother and sister, and called them both *Ramasse Poubelles*, the bin-pickers. She told me they spent their entire time rummaging through the bins at various recycling and refuse points, and taking their findings back to their house, which was full to bursting.

Another near-neighbour told me she had once encountered the sister up at St Loo and St Dongle, stripped down to bra and knickers and actually inside one of the bins so she could have a really good rummage. I'm not sure what the rural French expression for 'there's nowt so queer as folk' would be, but they certainly deserved the epithet. Luckily I didn't encounter her there. But nor did I see any sign of HRH.

By the sixth day, I was really getting worried. It was just so unlike her that I was beginning to fear the worst. Then I had a bright idea. The local radio station, France Bleu Pays d'Auvergne, broadcast some small ads each day, not just things for sale and wanted, but also dogs and cats lost and found. I thought I'd phone them and leave a message about HRH to be broadcast in the hopes that someone somewhere might have seen her or even taken her in.

I got through to the radio station and told them what I wanted. I was told I would be put through, so I mentally composed my advert whilst I was waiting, as I thought, for somebody to take down my details. The next thing I knew, I heard the voice of the radio presenter Nathalie Combre and realised that I was somehow live on French radio.

Clearing my throat frantically, I mumbled a '*bonjour*', whereupon Nathalie immediately said: '*Vous êtes anglaise? J'adore votre accent!*' (You're English? I love your accent!). I wasn't quite sure if I was being made fun of, but I managed to stumble through what I had rehearsed, missing part Siamese seal point pussy cat (the French here often call a cat *minou* or *minette* rather than *chat*) with blue eyes, wearing a little pink collar with a bell.

I managed to get in my line about her having '*le regard qui tue*', 'looks that kill', from a popular French song. Once seen, the icy sapphire blue glare of HRH was not easily forgotten. We had quite a little chat about the particular character of Siamese cats and their crosses, with their very individual characters.

I didn't know if it would do any good, but at least I had tried. Someone might just recognise the description. If nothing else, it had been a good opportunity to practise my French in a stressful and unplanned situation.

A couple of hours after my unexpected live broadcast on French local radio, I was playing in the garden with the dogs. Ci's favourite game was penalty shoot-out. He would stand in front of the big double gates, dancing on the spot with excitement, like a horse doing piaffe, whilst I tried to kick a ball or a squeaky toy past him. Fleur just loved fetch games, which she would play for hours.

She was normally very focused on her toy, to the exclusion of anything or anyone else, so I was surprised when she rushed down to the bottom of the garden, leaving her fetch toy behind. She stood in the corner, staring up across the fields towards St Loo and St Dongle, squeaking with excitement and bouncing up and down on the spot.

There was nothing in sight, so I had no idea what had

excited her so much. Then I heard what Fleur's super-sensitive ears had heard long before me. In the distance, very faintly, was the unmistakeable sound of a little bell, tinkling on a sparkly pink collar. Then, bounding over the fields from far away, came a seal-coloured object, heading straight as a die for the grottage.

Fleur was beside herself by now, leaping up and down on her back legs like a meerkat looking across the plains of Africa. She was still squeaking, and I could just imagine what those squeaks meant: 'She's coming, she's coming! Freddie's coming home!'

And she was. It was the princess herself, running as fast as her little velvet paws would carry her. She sped past the bottom of the garden and round to the entry into the cow byre, then flung herself up the ramp like a small ballistic missile.

I rushed across the garden, up the steps onto the top deck and into the hay loft to meet her. She had never been an affectionate cat but she was rubbing around my legs as if she was as delighted to be back as I was to see her safe.

She was very hungry but seemed otherwise perfectly fine, not injured or anything. What could have happened? Maybe she'd been shut in somewhere nearby all this time and someone had heard me on the radio, checked an outbuilding, and let her loose. Perhaps she'd even heard my voice herself and decided it was time to end the adventure.

I would never know, of course. I was just so relieved to have her back.

Chapter Fifteen
Happy Birthday

Jill had planned her annual visit in 2012 for July as usual, and it was going to be a special year for both of us; the year when we turned sixty. Of course, for much of our working life, we had been looking forward to that milestone year as the time when we could retire on our pensions. But things had changed dramatically. Retiring age was rising and we would both now have to wait until we were sixty two years and four months to qualify for a UK state pension and in Jill's case, a work-related pension which I wouldn't get, being self-employed.

There was a slight difficulty this year over me taking Jill back to the airport at the end of her week's stay. My symptoms of fatigue and nausea, although intermittent, were not getting any better. I'd been to and fro to my doctor and had endless blood tests. One of them finally threw up a clue as to what might be going on. There were abnormally high antibodies in my blood, which, the doctor said, could be a sign of coeliac disease. A biopsy of the small intestine would be required to confirm that or rule it out. Oh great, another close encounter of the worst kind with the bitey snake.

The appointment was fixed for the day of Jill's return flight so, much as I didn't really want to go for it, there wasn't much choice, I needed to get sorted out. Jill was more than happy to get a taxi, so I booked my near-neighbour, Alf, half of the duo from whom I had bought the grottage, who ran a taxi firm.

I knew next to nothing about coeliac disease, other than I'd once met someone who couldn't have soy sauce because of it. Doubtless there was a lot more to it than that, so I did some internet research. Some of the symptoms did tally with mine. Then I got to the list of things people with coeliac disease cannot eat. Wheat? Oh no, no more French bread, or *pain au chocolat!* That would be a total disaster, especially as the best baker in the area had just started a once-weekly home delivery to our hamlet. His *baguettes* were sublime, but his *pain au chocolat* really was to die for. There must be some mistake – I demand a recount!

The good news was that I was told not to make any changes to my diet before the next encounter with the bitey snake or it could mask the results of the biopsy which would be taken. This meant that for the week of Jill's visit, I could carry on eating as normal, as long as I felt up to it, and could enjoy plenty more *pains au chocolat.*

As usual, Jill and I would be spending a couple of days away somewhere during her visit and I had started scouting around for somewhere to camp. We'd done the mountainous, volcanic region of the Massif du Sancy a couple of times, so I thought it would be nice to explore a bit more of the Livradois-Forez region where I now lived.

Most weekends, I now took both dogs to class lessons with Caro, our wonderful trainer. Her training ground was up in the Haut Livradois and the area all around there was very attractive and new to both Jill and to me.

The camping season in this part of France is incredibly short. It seems it's only eccentric English people who want to go camping all year round. Some of the sites are only open in July and August. Very few open before Easter and most close by September. So my choice of ones to try out before Jill's visit in July was a bit limited.

I picked one in Marsac en Livradois simply because it was open, although the scenery in the area is not all that special. It was a Dutch-owned site, a small private one, and I hoped it would be a bit more welcoming than some Dutch sites I have stayed at where the owners don't even speak French and all the signs everywhere are in Dutch only.

What I didn't realise, because I have no interest at all in sports, is that I'd chosen a day when the Netherlands were playing France at football in some important match or another, perhaps even the World Cup. And as luck would have it, the pitch I'd been allocated for my tent was next to a caravan with big football fans, complete with orange curly wigs and vuvuzelas, supporting the Netherlands' team. What fun that was going to be for the night, especially if the Netherlands won their match.

I'm not completely anti-social on my camping trips. I don't mind chatting to people, but I do like a bit of peace and quiet, especially if I have a good book to read. I'm not too keen on people just wandering up and trying to talk, as Ci is a suspicious dog who's inclined to bark at strangers and Fleur copies him.

The orange-wigged woman from the next caravan had already tried to engage me in conversation so I'd exchanged a few polite words before going back to my book. Then she went off to the main house with her husband, as all the campers were going to join the site's hosts to watch the match together.

I gathered the Netherlands had not been successful when I heard a procession of not-so-happy campers trudging dejectedly back to their caravans. Although it was not late, I was snuggled up peacefully in my sleeping bag, reading my book, with my dogs curled up one on either side of me.

My neighbour was clearly bored and felt cheated of an evening's entertainment when her team had lost. Her next choice of sport appeared to be attempting to force a reluctant English woman out of her tent to come and play.

She came over and stood just outside my tent, which, of course, started the dogs off barking. She began by asking if I wanted to go and have a drink with her and her husband. I declined politely. She then suggested I go and have a meal. I declined, explained I was already in bed reading, thanked her and bade her goodnight.

Her invitations became more insistent until she said, and I could almost hear an accompanying stamp of the foot: 'But I want you to come out and talk to me.' I had to be most insistent that I did not want to, and even firmer in wishing her goodnight, before she eventually, and reluctantly, went back to her caravan.

Not just because of that, but because there was not much in the area, scenery-wise, to excite me, I crossed that particular camp-site off the list for Jill's visit.

Jill's flight from Southampton was on time and I met her at the airport. One of the first outings I'd arranged for us once she had arrived was a carriage drive round a farm and the surrounding lanes, to see the cattle and the beautiful countryside. I used to drive ponies myself so am extremely aware of how dangerous carriage driving can be in the hands of someone inexperienced.

As soon as we took our seats in the huge covered wagon and our lady coachman had taken up the reins, I knew we were in extremely safe hands. Just as well, considering each one of the two Breton horses pulling the wagon weighed about half a ton and the covered wagon itself weighed eight hundred kilos. And as, when the terrain allowed, she would spring the horses (allow them to canter on strongly) one false move on her part could have upturned the lot on top of us.

It was a fabulous way to see the scenery, with parts of the drive affording us amazing views to the distant town of Thiers, the cutlery capital. So picturesque, so unlike England's cutlery capital, Sheffield.

We had the weekend away, taking both dogs to their training class, where Jill worked Ci, who always behaved impeccably for her. From there we went on to a camp-site I had selected, not far from the dog training ground. We took my big two-bedroom tent with a living area, rather than the pop-up tents, so we had room to spread about.

As we were just getting sorted and settled, with the dogs sitting down being quite well behaved, we noticed that our caravan neighbours to one side also had a pet with them. Except theirs was a kitten, which was going to make for some fun as it kept wanting to come over and meet the dogs.

I'd noticed something about the French. They have an uncanny knack of being able to perform the seemingly impossible, to train cats to behave as well as dogs. Our neighbours at the site said they'd only had their young cat for a month or so but already they were able to let it out to go scampering round the camp-site amusing itself, and it would obediently come to call like a well-behaved dog when they wanted it to come back in.

My neighbour at the grottage was the same with her white cat Neige (snow). Like many white cats, Neige was quite deaf. Yet somehow, my neighbour had her trained to come when she rattled a box of cat treats.

Jill is exactly four days younger than I am and never lets me forget it. So for our sixtieth birthdays, I'd planned a bit of revenge. Through my friend Christine I'd discovered a very good bar- restaurant, the Bar Le St Thomas, at St Genès-la-Tourette. It was run by an English man and his South African wife and served really delicious home-cooked food. I'd booked us in there for lunch and had arranged with John and Pat to make a special big fuss of Jill for her birthday.

It was very pleasant and not too long a drive from the camp-site. On the map, we could see a viewpoint marked so decided to stop there to walk the dogs and see the view. French cartographers clearly have a sense of humour though, as, try as we might, we never did find the viewpoint, at least not where it was marked on the map.

Our lunch was wonderful, with party balloons, and Pat and

her daughter singing Happy Birthday at the table. We had delicious food and great fun. As is normal here, lunch was four courses, a starter, main course, then the cheese course, followed by dessert.

The day before Jill left, we had a tea party in the garden back at the grottage, with Patrick and his family and Geoff and Christine. I made scones, although I couldn't find clotted cream anywhere so we had to settle for whipped cream and jam. It was something our French friends had never before discovered and which went down very well. I ate as many as possible, in case it really was the last time I would be allowed to, although I was still convinced the blood test results were wrong and it would be something much less life-changing.

Then it was time for Jill to take her taxi to the airport and Christine once again to come and drive me to Thiers hospital for another encounter with the bitey snake. As this would now be my third time, I was more than a little apprehensive.

Especially as this time, the consultant was nearly half an hour late arriving, whilst I lay on the trolley in the procedure room and the nurses kept me chatting to keep my spirits up and my anxiety levels down. I'd been allowed to take medication this time to help me feel more relaxed but, of course, with the delay, the effects had more or less worn off by the time the consultant arrived.

It meant a false start, as when he began to pass the camera down my throat, for a moment I wasn't sure I could tolerate it and had to ask for a brief pause. And this time, as he was doing biopsies as well, once I did successfully manage to swallow the wriggling anaconda, it began biting chunks out of my stomach and small intestine, which was not at all pleasant.

I actually really like snakes. My plot of land across the road from the grottage is home to a large collection of enormous grass snakes, some adders, a few aspic vipers and some slow worms. I know slow worms are really legless lizards and not snakes but they do look wonderfully slithery and snake-like.

Once at the Pink House I'd managed to get myself bitten by an aspic viper. I'd gone into my mother's bedroom for something and saw just the end of a tail about to disappear under her wardrobe. For some reason, several of her carers were absolutely petrified of snakes so, without really thinking, I grabbed the tail before it disappeared.

The correct way to pick up a snake, if you have to, is, of course, by holding it directly behind the head, as that way it can't reach round to bite you. Holding only the tail meant the little viper could and did easily wriggle around and sink its dear little fangs into my hand several times before I could drop it out of the window and close it.

It was only small so presumably quite young so I just got my venom pump and vacuum sucked out any possible venom. There was no reaction at all, and on internet researching I found that some snakes don't release their venom on the first couple of bites which serve as a warning, so I had clearly been lucky.

At the grottage, an adder had taken up residence right outside the front door. It was a lovely place to bask in the sun on the warm decking, curled up against one of the door shutters. I didn't mind for me but it was too much of a worry for the dogs, so I carefully picked it up and carried it across the road to let it go near where the others were. The very next day it was back, so I let it stay, just keeping a careful eye on the dogs as they went past it. Based on nothing scientific, I decided it was a female and named it Hissing Cyd Charisse.

But it has to be said, I really didn't like the feel of that big snake sliding down my throat and biting lumps out of me whilst I retched and dribbled ,with my eyes streaming. At least it was over relatively quickly.

A couple of weeks later, I saw my own doctor who gave me the results of the biopsy. The villi in my small intestine, the little hair-like projections on the lining of the gut which aid digestion, were atrophied. I definitely had coeliac disease.

As sixtieth birthday presents go, it was not the best I could have had. Luckily it had been caught early so was perfectly manageable, as long as I excluded all traces of gluten from my diet for ever more. That meant no wheat, no rye, no barley and initially, no oats. Although they don't contain gluten, they do contain avenin, to which some coeliac sufferers can be sensitive.

It would mean, in effect, learning to bake all over again, since gluten is the substance which gives the classic consistency to bread, in particular. As I was to discover, rural central France was not really up to speed with the huge range of gluten-free products now available in UK supermarkets.

In a few of the nearest shops where I asked for gluten-free products I was met with a blank expression and was asked what gluten was. Sometimes I was asked if it was found in nuts. Eating out was going to be a bit of a nightmare. It was already hard enough as I don't eat meat, though will eat fish and fowl of necessity, and vegetarian meals are still very much a novelty in this area. But to be a meat-refusing coeliac didn't bear thinking about.

I discovered some gluten-free bread in one of the larger supermarkets and quickly discovered two things. First, it was about three times the price of ordinary bread and although I was theoretically entitled to a part reimbursement because of my social security payments, the form-filling was so complicated, I never did succeed. And two, it was so tasteless I would have been better throwing away the 'bread' and eating the packet it came in.

Friends in the UK were kind and well-meaning, but without knowing anything of life in the Livradois-Forez, their advice came across as patronising. Had I thought of using rice flour instead of wheat? Of course I'd thought of it, but not achieved it, because there was a decided lack of an Asian deli in Olliergues, population eight hundred and something. The supermarkets didn't have it; the health food shops did, but again, at a high price and a longer journey to source it than I'd hoped for.

I am a confirmed locavore, I like to shop in my local towns and villages but that was going to be impossible for many things. And of course, the French way of life revolves around the daily bread and the morning trip to the *boulangerie*. People tended not to bake their own bread so much, so it was harder to source good ingredients, and certainly good gluten-free ones.

Still, I'd got the diagnosis now. It was definite, there was no getting away from it. So I was just going to have to learn as much about my new best friend coeliac disease as I possibly could and start getting on with it, child. First, a trip to see a dietician for her advice. Next join both AFDIAG, the French Association of Gluten Intolerants, and Coeliac UK as well, to be sure of understanding everything I needed to. Then Google, and mercifully, picking the brains of Anne, a good friend on Twitter with two coeliac sons and a lot of common sense to impart.

Sixty years old. The start of a new era, and the start of a completely new lifestyle – without pain au chocolat.

Mother, was it worth it?

Chapter Sixteen
Bargain Hunting

Vide grenier (attic sale) season in rural France is an important part of the way of life. Depending on the weather in a particular region, there is something going on every weekend and most bank holidays from about Easter to the autumn, and in some places, they run all year.

They come in all shapes and sizes, from half a dozen stalls in a village square, to a few hundred stalls on a big field. There are *brocantes, vide greniers, marchés aux puces*, and *foires fouilles*, roughly speaking, second-hand markets, attic sales, flea markets and rummage sales. They are amazing places to find bargains and, following my diagnosis, one of my missions was to find myself an affordable second-hand bread machine with a gluten-free programme so I could have a go at making myself something which resembled bread.

One person's misfortune is definitely another's fortune. At one of the sales previously, I'd encountered an older English couple from one of the local villages. They were moving back to the UK, he reluctantly, she with much relief as she missed her family and the cost of return flights to visit them was eating into their savings.

I'd already had some great bargains from them, including two folding camping chairs with the extension part to put your feet up. I think I paid the outrageous sum of a euro each for those. The husband had helped me to carry them back to my van and had been chatting me up as we went. His wife later told me he did that to all the French speaking Brits he could find, as he was desperate to stay but despite his best efforts, he just could not make any in-roads into learning French.

Many expats are just bone idle, in my humble opinion and experience, and make no effort with the language. But because of my own struggles with slight dyscalculia, I readily accept there are those for whom a foreign language will forever remain just that – foreign. Try as I might, I cannot make sense of anything mathematical, so I understood that it would be the same for some with a foreign language.

I was thrilled to see the English couple again at a little rummage sale where I'd always found good bargains at great prices and, amazingly, in the centre of their table of offerings, was a bread machine! It looked in very good condition, it had a gluten-free programme and, best of all, they only wanted five euros for it – bargain! The slight problem was there were no instructions with it, but they were sure they had some somewhere, so I left them my telephone number and they promised to telephone me if the booklet came to light whilst they were packing up their home.

True to her word, the woman telephoned me a couple of days later and we arranged to meet up so I could pick up the instruction booklet and wish them all the best for their imminent move back to the UK. I really didn't envy them.

Armed with book and machine, I was all ready to have my first go at making an edible gluten-free loaf. I just needed to find the right flour. No chance at all in the Petit Casino in either Olliergues or Augerolles. Nothing, either, in the bigger Intermarché in Courpiere, although the stock manager there was very kind and helpful and said she was looking to expand her range for people with special dietary needs.

The next port of call was Thiers, where there was both a large Carrefour supermarket and a small health food shop. I wanted to check both out and compare prices. My first preference was always to support small local businesses, but there was a limit to how much I could afford to pay out to do so.

Health food shop first, as apart from anything, it was the only place I'd found where I could buy jars of molasses, an excellent natural source of iron. They had some bread mix, expensive, but I bought a bag to try. I loved going in the shop, it was filled with delicious healthy smells of spices. The woman who ran it was friendly and helpful, and would always try to get things in if she didn't have them and took a seemingly genuine interest in her customers and their health.

What a contrast in the Thiers branch of Carrefour. As large supermarkets go, Carrefour is not a bad one; perhaps the French equivalent of Tesco in the UK. But that particular branch has to rate as the worst I have ever visited. There are never enough checkouts open, ever, no matter what time of day you go, or which day of the week. The customer service personnel who are supposed to be there to help you are totally disinterested. If you ask for a particular product, their first, and usually only, response is to ask if you have looked for it on the shelves. Some people maintain that all customer service in France is like that. I must be lucky, as I haven't encountered that attitude in other shops.

But they did, at least, have gluten-free flour, and much cheaper than the health food shop, although of course theirs was not organic, as my earlier purchase has been.

So armed with bags of flour and bread mix, I rushed home to my bargain purchase, looking forward to having some proper bread again.

I followed the instructions carefully, weighed everything, used the ingredients at room temperature, as the recipe suggested, then waited. So why did the object which emerged at the end of the baking cycle resemble a house brick? I could probably have repaired part of the crumbling wall in the old cow byre with it.

To misquote, as I often do, Dr 'Bones' McCoy, from the first series of Star Trek: 'It's bread, Jim, but not as we know it.'

It wasn't the bread machine's fault, that remained a really good bargain. I later discovered the tip to a good consistency was to add a teaspoonful of vinegar to the dough. It never did taste like real bread, more like a tea loaf, or a fruit loaf without the fruit. But it was edible, and much cheaper than the awful stuff on offer in the shops.

It was amazing what bargains you could pick up at the *vide greniers*. Like my mother before me, I simply can't resist a bargain. I now had more clothes then I could ever wear in a lifetime, especially as some were very nice and quite formal. The opportunity for formal wear in this rural area, with my lifestyle, was limited indeed. But if I saw a beautifully tailored designer linen two-piece, trouser suit of course, since I never wear skirts, for just four euros, it would be criminal to leave it, wouldn't it?.

I would never be cold again, either, thanks to my expanding collection of warm winter jackets. Well, genuine Pyrenean goose down in a padded jacket, almost new, for five euros – who wouldn't want that?

There would often be food vans at the sales, delicious dishes like crêpes which were now off limits to me, of course. I would just have to get used to carrying my own snacks with me wherever I went. Of course there was almost always a bar as no such occasion in France would be complete without wine.

Shabby chic was as much all the rage in France as in the UK, and lots of French loved *chiner*, to hunt for antiques. With a good eye and haggling skills, there were great bargains to be found amongst the tat.

The French also didn't seem to have the same paranoia about selling electrical goods as has taken over in the UK. I bought several gadgets including a mini blender for making smoothies, or 'smoozees' as the French call them, for less than a euro, untested, uncertified, and to date, none of them has electrocuted me.

Not that I was becoming addicted, of course, but once the sales were on, my weekly plans revolved round them and their location. There was a website which I consulted to find what was on where, but it was still necessary to keep your eyes peeled whilst driving around as some of the smaller ones didn't advertise online. You had to watch out for signs appearing at the side of the road, as sometimes the smaller ones had the best bargains.

Olliergues, my little local town, had a really good one, just a few stalls, but I got lots of really nice stuff. On one stall I spotted the classic French man bag, the leather document bag on a shoulder strap which so many men carried. I thought it would be really useful for me when I didn't need to take much with me so I asked the price. The stall-holder was keen to clear her stall so she could go home so she said one euro. Before I could even get a coin out of my purse, she produced another similar one, also in leather, and said I could have the two for a euro.

There was another temptation to the sales. I had discovered an enterprising English woman who went round markets and sales with her van, selling English sweets. The French were intrigued by the delights of such specialities as Kendal mint cake, which I absolutely loved.

It took me back to the weekends of my youth when a favourite activity would be to board the number twenty-eight bus from the top of the road with friends, ride it to Hayfield, walk over the top of the Dark Peak into Edale and come back on the train. There was always Kendal mint cake in our rucksacks and it was usually consumed before the bus had got up the first hill into Marple.

Another blast from the past that I was rediscovering was Cadbury's Chocolate Éclairs – delicious! Sadly, all that was to change because of five little words: 'may contain traces of gluten.' People with a gluten intolerance can often cope with the dreaded 'traces of'. Sadly, coeliac is not an allergy or an intolerance but an autoimmune disease, for which the tolerance level is twenty parts per million. In other words, not even 'traces of'.

But at least the English sweetie lady had the kindness to sell some delicious fudge which was completely gluten-free, so I could still frequent her stall.

My dogs loved me going to the *vide greniers*. Both were very toy focused and loved nothing better than pouncing on and mauling cuddly toys. I could pick them up by the armful for pennies, or centimes, rather, so they would have great fun racing round the garden killing their latest trophy.

Of course there were a few disasters amongst my bargain purchases along the way, inevitably. I was really pleased with a pair of Quechua walking boots, just my size, which seemed in really good condition. I wore them on a walk with the dogs and they seemed fine.

However when I got back in the van and started driving, I wondered why I was having difficulty managing the pedals with my feet. Then I looked down and saw that on each boot, the sole had completely peeled away from the boot's upper, like pulling back the skin of a banana. Oops! Still, only four euros down the drain, and with Baden Powell 'Be Prepared' training, I always had a spare pair of walking boots in the van.

The sales were also a great way to explore the local countryside, and through the sales website, I was discovering towns and villages I might not otherwise have come across. For those further afield I would sometimes take the tent and camp over, if it was not too hot to leave the dogs in the van. They were a bit of a boisterous handful to tow round a sale, or rather, to be towed round by.

From time to time when my wardrobes and drawers were groaning at the seams too much, I would have a clear out and recycle some stuff to one of the charity bins which were slowly starting to appear round and about, though nothing like as widespread as in the UK.

Through the winter months, I looked forward almost as much to the return of the *vide greniers* as I did to the sounds of the returning birds; the first cuckoo, the distinctive hoop-hoop-hoop of the hoopoes and the intricate fluting call of the golden orioles.

Chapter Seventeen
Frogification

The British have long referred to the French as Frogs or Froggies. It comes from a long-standing urban myth that all French people eat frogs' legs, most of the time. It's no more true of the French than their own nickname for the British, *les rosbifs*, roast beefs. Despite what many people think, it's not derived from dietary origin, it is instead a reference to the British habit, less so in these enlightened times, of arriving in a sunny country, stripping off and sunbathing until they were burnt as red as a piece of under-done beef.

I hadn't yet encountered anyone who ate frogs' legs on more than the odd occasion and had only seldom seen them on a menu in a restaurant. But the age-old nickname had stuck and would probably always stick.

Even before I had bought my own place, I had already made up my mind that I wanted to remain in France. Because I don't believe in doing things by halves, I decided I wanted to take French citizenship. In other words, I wanted to be Frogified.

As a citizen of Europe, I had the right of residence in France, and no longer needed the old *carte de séjour*, residency permit, to live there. But I was not convinced that Britain would remain a member of Europe indefinitely. I no longer specifically followed the British news or its politics, but I saw things on the internet which concerned me.

People said I was crazy, it would never happen. Until I reminded them that, until 2010, they would not have believed that Britain would have an unelected government in power. My firm belief is that anything can happen in politics, and that sometimes the protest vote can result in all sorts of mischief.

I had now been in France the requisite five years in order to start my application process. I knew that it was very often a long and complicated procedure. Patrick and Cecilia warned me of friends of theirs who had been waiting for years for their citizenship. But they were from outside the European Union, so I hoped that, as a citizen of Europe, things might go a little more quickly for me, despite the legendary slow grindings of French bureaucracy.

One of the requirements for the application was to have passed a recognised language examination in French at intermediate level within the last two years. My French was reasonably good by now, I managed in most situations, but I like to give my very best effort to anything I do – it's the Leo in me. I decided I needed some lessons to brush up.

The most geographically convenient language school for me was in Vichy, which is where I would be sitting the exam. But the prices for lessons were really high – I needed to find something much more within my budget.

By chance, I hit on a cunning plan. The tourist offices in the Livradois-Forez all ran lots of guided walks and talks through the spring and summer. There were historical discovery walks around towns, walks to learn about medicinal wild plants, walks on top of the Hautes Chaumes, the wild and protected upland heaths, moors and grasslands, to discover the flora and fauna.

Many were free. At most, they cost about six euros for two hours or more of listening to French being spoken. All were subjects which interested me greatly. It seemed a wonderful way to brush up my French listening skills, whilst doing something I would really enjoy.

I signed up for everything. Often, the turnout was so low I would be the only one with the guide. I visited the museum in Olliergues and saw how wooden clogs were made. I did the historic tour of the town and learned about its heritage as a producer of sails for the French navy.

In Southampton (Cunlhat, remember?) I spent two and a half hours alone with a guide who took me on a walking tour round the many fountains in the town, finishing with a visit to a fascinating small private museum which most tourists would never see the inside of.

On the medicinal plant walk, with a woman who would certainly be branded as a hedge witch, I learned the old French remedy of drinking an infusion of ash leaves to ease arthritic pain. It works, too – I still make my own.

On a bat walk, I discovered that the Auvergne has more species of bats than anywhere else in France, possibly in Europe, and we were privileged to see several of them. Our guide showed us that by carefully tossing a tiny pebble near to a bat, it would instantly alter its flight trajectory to swoop after it, and investigate if it was edible.

On another wild plant walk, we finished up at the home of the Bowing Farmer, where he kindly let us wash the various plants we had collected so we could taste some of them. I still didn't discover his name, though, as he had no letter box at the end of the driveway for me to check.

Back up on the Hautes Chaumes I learned the names of the various lizards and butterflies which lived there. Our guide picked up a common viviparous lizard to show us. It seemed perfectly unconcerned by our interest, almost as if posing for the public on these guided walks was part of its job.

I was very pleased with myself on that particular walk. As we walked past a field of cows, several of the people present asked our guide why one of the cows was wearing a spiky plastic ring through her nose. Our guide didn't know, but because my best friend Jill teaches agriculture and I had recently asked her the same question, I did. I was able to tell the group it was because she tried to suckle from the other cows and this would ensure she was butted out of the way. I managed to explain it in French, although I did lack some of the vocabulary!

The walks were brilliant for me, they involved intense listening and concentrating, and afforded the opportunity to ask questions and interact. They were fascinating and I learned so much about the heritage of my adopted region. Best of all, they cost me very little.

It had been a long time since I had taken any sort of exam. I wanted to prepare myself as fully as I could so that I didn't lose marks through not knowing what I was supposed to be doing. In particular, I wanted to find exactly what form the exam would take. Apart from anything, it was costing me seventy-five euros. I didn't want to have to pay for a re-sit if I failed by not being properly prepared. I bought a CD and a book to tell me exactly what I was letting myself in for.

Luckily the exam for the citizenship application does not require any written French. Just as well, as I can disguise my grammatical faults well enough when I speak it, but they would be all too plain in writing. It consisted of a comprehension exercise, listening to and answering thirty questions in twenty-five minutes, then a one to one interview with an examiner, answering six questions.

The required pass mark was level three, intermediate, but in both sections of the exam, questions would cover levels one to six, beginner to advanced. The more difficult the question, the more marks it was worth. So if you did fluff the early ones through lack of concentration, it was still theoretically possible to obtain a pass mark by answering the more difficult ones correctly.

I was so pleased I had invested in the CD and book, as the actual way of answering the oral section was a bit complicated. Like so many exams these days, it was a multiple choice one.

The questions were all on a disc which would be played in the examination room, with no repetitions; the answers were on a sheet of paper. Sometimes you simply ticked a box numbered from one to four after listening to proposed answers. Sometimes four possible written answers were given and you had to tick the correct one.

I practised hard every day. The more difficult questions sometimes involved a paragraph being read whilst you frantically tried to guess what the statements to come might be, to be ready to tick the correct one on the sheet. Inevitably, they were never the questions you thought they might be.

As well as passing the exam, there was a small lorry load of paperwork to be prepared for the dossier which was sent to the Ministry of the Interior with the application form. I'd been to the *sous-préfecture* to collect the form from the woman in charge of residency and citizenship. The *préfectures*, or their sub-departments, represent national government at local level in France and are responsible for such roles as issuing driving licences and vehicle registrations as well as work and residency permits.

The woman I saw was a bit abrupt and had rather the air of dealing with a very unpromising school pupil who had suddenly expressed a desire to sit a scholarship exam for a top university.

She handed me a pile of paperwork, pointed out what was what and what was required, then sent me on my way, clearly thinking she had a better chance of being elected as the new Pope as I had of managing to get together all the various documents I would need.

But my motto has always been 'I like a challenge', so I dutifully carried home all the *paperasse*, the paperwork. The Brits often call it 'bumf', many without knowing that it's a military slang term meaning 'bum fodder', which accurately sums up many people's opinions on form-filling.

Because I'm superstitious, I was reluctant to start filling in too many of the forms before I knew if I would pass the French exam. It seemed somehow to be tempting fate. But there was an enormous amount to do, so I knew I would have to make a start.

In particular, French authorities will seldom accept documents such as birth certificates in their original language, not even when they are fairly simple and include vocabulary no more challenging than 'father's name', 'mother's name'. Also they won't accept a translation from just any professional translator, it must be from a court certified one.

So all of my documents, birth certificates for me and my parents, marriage certificates, death certificates for them, divorce decree for me, all had to be sent for translation, all adding to the cost. Once all the documents were gathered together, with the French exam certificate, should I manage to pass, there was a fiscal stamp to be bought – they're sold in *tabacs*, tobacconists' shops, or cafés with a cigarette counter – and identity photos to be added, then the whole dossier would be taken back to the *sous-préfecture* and handed in to the strict and sceptical woman in charge.

But first there was the exam to be tackled. I'd received my timings; I had to be there at two o'clock for the comprehension section, but my oral exam was not until nearly six o'clock, which meant a lot of waiting round.

As usual, I arrived far too early, but it did mean I found a convenient parking space directly outside the language school. The foyer was filling up with exam candidates. I found a seat next to a young woman from Portugal, and we chatted in French whilst we waited, for the practice.

There were about forty candidates when we were finally all ushered into the exam room, sitting in rows, in individual desks, just like being back at school. The invigilator explained the procedure and showed us how to use the answer sheets in front of us, then started the CD of questions.

The first ones, the level one questions, were extremely

easy, and there were a few quiet snorts of laughter at how simple they were. Then they started to increase in difficulty as we went through the levels.

My problem was not one of comprehension but of concentration. I've always found a disembodied voice hard to focus on. I've always preferred television to radio since I need the visual clues as well, and I'm very easily distracted when it comes to ... oh look, a butterfly. You get the idea.

Some of the candidates, despite being fluent French speakers, were struggling with how to use the multiple choice answer form. Those of us of a certain age had never encountered them in our school days. The invigilator was very kind, miming what to do to those who struggled the most.

I understood everything but for me the hardest was to listen to a passage being read, then listen to the four possible answers then remember which number was the correct one to tick off on the sheet. But I made it to the end, not without a big sigh of relief.

The exam is supposed to show that candidates are capable of conducting themselves in normal day-to-day situations. Of course an exam setting is totally artificial, compared to everyday life, where one can ask for things to be repeated, or ask for an explanation of an unfamiliar word.

Now I had the long wait before the next part of the exam. There was a real ethnic mix of candidates present, many from North Africa plus a lot from various regions of Europe. I appeared to be the only Brit. I sat and chatted to the Portuguese woman plus others from the Netherlands, Russia and Switzerland, all of us speaking French as our common language of choice.

I was the last candidate for the oral exam, the disadvantage of coming low down on any list alphabetically. An examiner came and took me to a room and explained that our question and answer session would be recorded.

The questions began very easily, starting with stating basic facts like name and address and progressed through expanding on ideas and expressing opinions. At one point I was required to interview the examiner, a piece of cake for a former journalist, even in a foreign language. As far as I knew, I only stumbled over one word, 'embrace', in the sense of embracing a new culture. I wasn't sure if, in my enthusiasm, I had said I wanted to kiss French culture. But I think I managed to convey the correct meaning by paraphrasing, and a later quick check in the dictionary showed I had been right the first time.

Then followed an anxious wait of a couple of weeks to see if I had passed. It was necessary to pass both sections of the exam at a minimum of level three to get an overall pass. If you failed one section, you failed overall, even if you had passed the other section at the highest level, level six.

Whilst waiting for my results, I didn't want to touch my dossier at all, in case it meant bad luck. Not very scientific, but still.

Then finally the brown envelope arrived. With trembling fingers, I opened it and took out the single sheet of stiff paper.

A pass in both sections, and both above the required level! So now I could start on the bumf and get my application in.

Chapter Eighteen
Red Tape

French certificate safely in my hot little hand, it was time to throw myself wholeheartedly into getting the rest of my citizenship application sorted out.

All the official translation documents were now ready. I was determined to make my dossier exemplary, the best piece of homework Madame at the *sous-préfecture* had seen from one of her seemingly less promising applicants. I'd previously worked as both a case tracker for the Crown Prosecution Service and a filing clerk in an army headquarters so I knew a thing or two about efficient filing.

I bought myself a plastic folder with different sections, labelled each according to the documents required, and started to assemble everything. I included absolutely everything they had asked for and a few extras which I hoped might enhance my chances. So that they wouldn't think I was planning to sponge off the state, I included details of my meagre savings, such as they were.

It was coming up to Christmas when I finally had my smart dossier all neatly filed away into easy sections. I even printed out an index to put at the front, with the documents which were to be found in each section. I was ridiculously proud of my efforts.

By now the weather was turning decidedly snowy, but I didn't want to leave my handiwork until the new year so I struggled through the snow to take it to Ambert. I hoped that might be a point in my favour – the intrepid English woman so keen to get her application in that she battles through snowy roads and icy footpaths to deliver it.

I saw the same woman again and this time, she actually looked quite impressed with my project. To my dismay, she took everything out of my carefully prepared folder and jumbled it all up on her desk to check everything was present, before handing me back the empty folder.

But at least I had delivered my application. The next step was to be interviewed by the secretary general at the *sous-préfecture* as to my suitability to be Frogified. An appointment was duly made for the following week, the day after Christmas Day, since Boxing Day does not exist in France and only Christmas Day itself is a public holiday.

One thing I knew the French were very keen on in considering the application was to see signs of integration into French life. Applications from people who didn't mix, or had the majority of their family in another country and kept up strong connections there, were not generally favourably looked upon.

Unfortunately one of the ways of assessing this was to ask what clubs and societies an applicant belonged to. I have never been a joiner. I'm not really a club sort of a person. I considered myself pretty well integrated. I belonged to the library and went often, I did all the guided walks, I was becoming known to the shopkeepers and stallholders in the area since I shopped as locally as I could. But I didn't have an impressive list of chess club, line dancing club, martial arts club and the like I could trot out.

The interview went well. I always found it an enormous advantage to be able to say I was not one hundred per cent British, because of my grandmother from Luxembourg. I found it was always well received, and also explained my accent, which I have often been told sounds like a Dutch or German person speaking French.

We came to the bit about clubs and organisations. I mentioned being an active member of the library in Olliergues, then said I attended the dog club every week, with my two dogs. It was stretching a point slightly, as it was not a club, as such, and not run as one. But I was a regular member and had been since it started.

The secretary general asked me if I held any office in the club, which would have been difficult, as it was not officially a club. Quickly I replied with an enigmatic: 'Not yet,' as if it were only a matter of time, which seemed to satisfy him. He said he would add his report, which would be favourable, to my dossier, before it was sent on to the ministry.

He also said that I would be interviewed by the police who would in turn have made local enquiries, especially with the mayor, to see if anything adverse was known about me.

I'd had to produce a copy of my criminal record from the UK, or rather my lack of one, as I was squeaky clean. I'd even managed to avoid coming to the attention of the French police, since arriving in the country, having not even picked up a driving fine.

A few days later, I was just arriving back at my house after my usual Saturday morning foray to the library and the fruit and veg market stall in the village. Having completely forgotten what I'd been told, I had a heart-stopping moment at seeing a *Gendarmerie* vehicle outside my front gate.

As I pulled up and got anxiously out to see what I had done wrong, two very smart young *gendarmes*, a man and a woman, got out of their vehicle. The man did the talking, the woman just stood by giving me a hard stare as if she thought I was probably some master criminal.

He said they had come to ask me some questions in connection with my citizenship application. I asked if they wanted to come into the house, praying that it wasn't, as usual, inches deep in mud and dog hair, but as it was a fine day, they said they could just ask the questions where we were.

They were more or less the same questions I'd been asked at the *sous-préfecture:* why I wanted to take French nationality, how often did I visit the UK – their eyebrows raised when I said never since I'd arrived in the Auvergne – what clubs did I belong to. Once again I trotted out the white lie about 'dog club' and said I would be heading off there as soon as I had put the shopping away.

Once again they declared themselves satisfied and said they would be putting in a favourable report. They said they had spoken to the mayor who was also in favour.

One of the nice things about rural French life here is that small communities do make the effort to welcome incomers of all nationalities. Soon after I arrived, I was invited to attend a reception given by the mayor for all the new residents, plus several key figures in the community.

As the *salles des fêtes*, the town's festival hall, was being refurbished, it was held at the secondary school. The mayor came and introduced himself to each of the new arrivals in turn and, certainly in my case, took pains to ask about the pronunciation of my name.

When everyone had arrived, all the newbies had to go to the front of the hall, facing the rest of the audience, and as we were introduced, one by one, by the mayor, we had to make some sort of gesture to make ourselves known. It was rather charming and once again, rather like the first day at school.

Then there was a short film show all about the town and what was going on in and around it, followed by the inevitable French buffet of cheese, ham, bread, wine and various other cheesy pastry nibbles.

So now my dossier was complete, with all the forms filled in, everything translated, the interview forms added and so on. It was on its way to the ministry, but it could be up to two years before I would get their response. I sincerely hoped it would not be a rejection, which they were perfectly entitled to do, as that would then mean my language exam certificate would have expired and I would have to start all over again.

French bureaucracy is legendary. Even the French themselves admit it is slow, cumbersome and extremely frustrating. I was starting to form an altogether different opinion. I decided that French *fonctionnaires*, civil servants and local government officers, actually did have a sense of humour, albeit a very individual one.

I knew my dossier was in order as I had been painstaking in its preparation and the woman official had checked it thoroughly before sending it off. I had supplied the requisite official translations of everything which required translation. So I was surprised and a bit aggrieved when, a few months after the dossier had gone in, I received a letter from the ministry. In it, they asked for the originals of my English birth and marriage certificates, and divorce decree. Not only did they already have officially translated copies of them all, they also had photocopies of the originals, exactly as was specified on the application form.

But as I joked with my neighbour, I had a theory about the request. I had decided that the *fonctionnaires* got bored, working away at their desks all day, so had invented a little game to play amongst themselves. They would think up the most improbable things to ask of applicants and see which of them would respond.

Perhaps they had a points system, whereby those getting a positive response to the most unlikely demand would win whatever was in the kitty that week. I imagine the one handling my dossier probably won. The conversation probably went something like this:

'Look, here's a mad English woman whose dossier is absolutely one hundred per cent complete and perfect. What can I ask her for that she's not already included?'

'Why not ask her for the originals of all her documents in English, now she's spent a fortune on getting them all translated into French?'

'Surely no-one would fall for that one, it's a bit far-fetched.'

Then, a few weeks later: 'Oh no, look, she fell for it, hook, line and sinker!! The fool! So all you guys owe me a *vin rouge* after work tonight.'

Oh well. I'd now given them absolutely everything they could reasonably, or unreasonably, have asked for. I could do nothing more except wait for their judgement. In the meantime, I resolved to keep my head down, keep paying all my taxes and social security contributions and stay out of any kind of trouble.

Roo the Kangoo was not a speedy vehicle at the best of times, but I was careful to lift my foot at the entrance to every town and village to avoid so much as a speeding fine. The actual name sign at the entrance to a town marks the start of the speed restriction in France, another peculiarity which can catch out the unwary foreigner.

I was determined to do nothing at all which might jeopardise my application. In the meantime, all I could do was wait.

Chapter Nineteen
Exploring Further

The Auvergne region is made up of four *départements,* the Allier, the Haute-Loire, the Cantal, and the Puy de Dôme, the one in which I lived. I had visited all of them but tended to stick to the Puy de Dôme as there was so much of it still to see and it was now my home.

As part of my drive to improve my French, however, I had ventured into the Haute-Loire on a little jaunt on the tourist railway. In the heyday of the railways, a busy branch line ran down the Dore valley, where Olliergues was situated, and up to La Chaise Dieu, the site of a Benedictine abbey, which was secularized during the French revolution.

Now only tourist trains used the rails and because of the cost to a small preservation society of maintaining the tracks, they no longer ran from Olliergues, but from Ambert, further south down the line. There were several different locomotives which made the trip, and there was a guide to give a running commentary on the journey.

Locomotives included a small steam train and one curious engine on which the driver sat perched high up on the roof in a tiny cab. But I chose a trip when the train was a *Panoramique*. These rail cars were built by Renault in 1959 and the one running on this line was the last of its kind in service. There was an upper deck with a bubble roof to give the best possible views. I got there in good time to be certain of a seat upstairs.

When I arrived at the ticket office to book my seat, I was told that there would be a slight delay on the return trip as there was a pre-booked trip on another train coming down the line and they had to leave a safe margin between the trains. We would, in fact, be delayed by half an hour.

I was a bit anxious as it was already a longish time to leave the dogs and because of his wonky bladder, Ci sometimes needed to go out quite often. But he was currently fine and I really wanted to do the trip so I decided I would go for it.

Rural France has an entirely different attitude to health and safety than does the UK. Things happen here which would cause an 'elf and safety' inspector in the UK to have a heart attack, but it was just accepted as the norm. Perhaps there were even fewer accidents because people were not constantly being mollycoddled and were instead expected to take a degree of responsibility for their own safety.

So I should not have been surprised that, rattling our way briskly along the tracks and hurtling up steep inclines and over high viaducts, the train doors were left open because it was hot, and children were happily running up and down the train. Because it was a two-storey train, that included racing up and down the steps that separated the two decks.

Nobody told them to go and sit down, not the guide giving the running commentary, and certainly not their parents. It wasn't that they were badly behaved, they were just being exuberant children, and none of them fell down the steps nor fell out of the open doors.

It was a wonderful journey, with some fantastic views, especially as we got nearer to La Chaise Dieu and could see the abbey perched on top of the thousand metre butte.

At the small station, we were greeted by a few stallholders selling local produce like jams, honey and spiced bread. There were samples to taste but, of course, the bread was now off limits to me.

All the train passengers headed off to walk the short

distance to the fourteenth century abbey, with its impressive Gothic architecture. Jill and I had previously visited it on our voyage of discovery around the Auvergne before I had moved there, so I just revisited the bits which were free admission, then had a walk round the town. It was a hot afternoon so I treated myself to a bowl of that French speciality, salted butter caramel ice cream. Delicious!

My fellow passengers and I all dutifully arrived back at the station a good half hour before our scheduled later departure time. I was a bit dismayed to see that the train which was holding up our departure was still at the platform and there was no sign of its party of passengers. As there needed to be a half hour safety margin between the two trains because of the steep downhill gradient, this was a little worrying. It meant our departure could well be an hour later than planned rather than half an hour.

Since all of the passengers from our train were now assembled on the platform, and only one or two from the other train had yet trundled slowly up the hill from the abbey, a few of us asked our guide if our train could not go first, instead of waiting. It would involve a little shifting and shunting of the trains, but the drivers seemed in agreement and went off to do so.

Soon we were all able to re-board our *Panoramique* whilst the other train was relegated to a siding. As we pulled out of the station, we were able to smirk smugly at the late-comers who now faced a wait of more than half an hour before they could begin their journey.

The descent involved a lot of squealing of brakes to regulate the train's speed as it hurtled its way back down to Ambert. I was heartily relieved to be in the front train, with a half-hour head start on the one following. We were soon safely back at the station, and I was back home in good time to let the dogs out before Ci became desperate for a *pipi*.

The *département* with the lowest population in the

Auvergne is the Cantal, in the south-west of the region. I was thinking ahead to future visits from Jill and from an old and dear friend Alex, who was hoping to come the following summer, and was looking for places for our little trips away.

One of my students, when I ran an English conversation group whilst living at the Pink House, had told me about the Cézallier plateau, which she said was very beautiful, isolated and under-populated, all of which sounded good to me. It was at the southern end of the Puy de Dôme, spilling over the boundary into the Cantal.

I headed down there with the dogs at the end of the season, just before the small municipal camp site I had selected online closed for the winter. It was the perfect site for us. It was on the side of a steep hill, with the tent pitches being on grassy terraces, and they were of a generous size. As there were so few people about at that time of year, we effectively had one whole terrace to ourselves, which comprised three big pitches and some picnic tables.

My student had told me there was a nature reserve near to where I was camping, at a place called La Godivelle, which had two lakes, one volcanic, one glacial. The area boasted good bird-life and an important expanse of peat-bog with rare plants, including carnivorous ones. There were plenty of big raptors, like short-toed eagles, and there had been recent sightings of osprey. Interesting, since it was no distance at all from a large wind farm, which didn't seem to affect the migrating birds at all.

The scenery was amazing, great wide expanses of open pasture land with barely any signs of habitation. I knew these pastures were the '*estives*', the summer grazing for the cattle, but they had now gone back down to the lower-lying fields, as summer was over and winter could arrive with sudden ferocity at any time now on the Massif Central.

I spotted a poster advertising a cattle sale at a little place called Brion, which I thought would be fun to go and see. As is often the way round here, no time was given for the event, it was presumed you had local knowledge. I went in the morning.

The place was easy enough to find, perched on top of a high plateau, and was both intriguing and charming. There was a row of small, stone-built constructions which turned out to be little restaurants, only open on sales days. The overall effect was like the fake village built in Ireland for David Lean's film 'Ryan's Daughter', a big favourite of mine.

There was not a sign of a single cow, although I found the cattle pens to the rear of the little restaurants. I found out later the actual sale was at silly o'clock in the morning, sparrow's fart, around five o'clock. But once the beasts were all sold and shipped to their new destinations, the farmers filled up the mini-inns and bistros to eat, drink and talk about cattle.

As the sale wasn't on, I decided to go for a drive around, over the border into the Cantal. Yet more beautiful scenery, hardly a house to be seen and so little traffic it was as if I had somehow missed the end of the world and was now the only person left.

Birds of prey were everywhere, probably filling up with good meals before they started their long flight back home for the winter. I stopped the van several times for a close-up look at the big short-toed eagles as they hung in the air, maintaining a down draft with fluttering wing beats. Red kites and buzzards were two a penny.

I was looking for a focal point for a dog walk and found myself following a sign to the *Lac des Estives*, the summer pastures lake. A long approach road led through fields and opened out to a parking area at a *gîte* and holiday chalet complex, with a large fishing lake. There was a reception area with a restaurant, which was advertising home-made ice cream.

I love ice cream! Especially home-made, as it meant I would be able to check on all the ingredients for any gluten contamination. In its absence, I could indulge in an enormous bowlful. But first, my dogs needed a walk, which meant negotiating our way round an enormous grey and white Pyrenean mountain dog who seemed to want to say hello to my two hooligans, who were more intent on a punch-up.

We had a wander around to see what the place was like. As well as the dining area, there was a large converted barn which had a *gîte* at one end and an exhibition room, with things about wolves and local legends about them, at the other end. It looked fascinating, but was currently closed.

A track led down to the chalets, and to the fishing lake. The upper chalets were permanent structures, the sort of concrete slab bungalows and dormer bungalows that could be thrown up in a very short space of time. They had all the featureless character of army married quarters and were packed quite close together. There was a large covered swimming pool at the end of where they stood.

Next down the track was the lake, of about seven acres in surface area. On the far side of it, nestled into the woods, was a cute little log cabin for rent, well removed from all the other chalets. The rest of the chalets were still further down the track and were delightful. They were like large garden sheds, each with a small decked sitting area outside, fenced round. Each one was painted in different whacky hippy colours, all two-tone. Bright yellow clashed gloriously with scarlet, vivid royal blue came to life with a trim of daffodil. Each had their own little parking area. Most had something of a view. All was quiet and peaceful, and the advantage of the ones at the bottom was that the track went no further, so there was no through traffic, a boon with barking dogs to think of.

I decided I had probably found the destination for trips away with Jill and with Alex, but there was still an acid test the establishment had to pass. Would its home-made ice cream be up to standard?

It was quiet, with no other holidays-makers around, as I left the dogs in the van and went into the dining area. The boss himself came out of the office area, casually dressed in zip-offs. We shook hands, as was customary. I enquired about the ice cream and its provenance, then settled on a big bowl of vanilla, my favourite, and some strawberry.

The moment of truth, as I lifted the first spoonful to my mouth. The deal-maker. If it was as good as it looked, I would be coming here on minibreaks with Jill and later with Alex.

As the French say, '*miam-miam*' (yum-yum). It really was delicious. I asked the boss, whose name was Alain, for some brochures and tariffs – a quick glance showed the prices to be reasonable, comparable to similar places.

I had found the venue for our next adventures away from the grottage.

Mission accomplished.

Chapter Twenty
Get Your Kit Off

French healthcare is undoubtedly of a high standard, generally speaking. Certainly all of my experiences to date had been positive. Although of course, I hadn't greatly enjoyed the encounters with the bitey snake.

One big difference between France and the UK, though, was being expected to get your kit off without turning a hair. Even alone with a male doctor, you are expected to strip off to your pants, sometimes altogether. Chaperone? No chance.

I've never been a prude. Never having had much in the bust department, I've never had much to be all that modest about. But I did find the attitude a little uncomfortable at times.

I'd first encountered it when I was summoned for a routine boob squashing session, a mammogram. Clearly when having breasts screened, one expects to have to expose them, also when the doctor comes to examine them and discuss any findings. But I feel the cold, quite a lot, so having to sit around for some time wearing nothing but my kecks and a smile was not my favourite occupation.

Similarly when I went for an ultra-sound scan of my abdomen, before the coeliac diagnosis, I'd found it all a bit relaxed, which took some getting used to. I was ushered into a small treatment room, and left to strip down, theoretically, to bra and pants, but as I don't even possess a bra, let alone wear one, it was a stretchy little crop top, and then lie down on the treatment couch.

That was fine, no problems there. But the radiographer who was to do the scan was delayed and it turned out the treatment room was some sort of rat-run for medical staff to take a short cut through. A seemingly constant procession of medical personnel trotted through, whilst I lay there in my underwear. All, of course, said the customary polite 'Bonjour, madame' as they passed through, but it was a strange feeling, and one I had never encountered in more prudish UK medical establishments where one was usually given at least a light blanket with which to cover ones modesty.

The various medical tests I had undergone had revealed a slight heart murmur, of which I was unaware. As all three of my mother's brothers had died of heart attacks, and my mother had had a history of angina and a leaky heart valve, my doctor advised me to go and get my heart checked out, although she hastened to assure me that my murmur was slight and unlikely to be anything serious.

But it was worth checking, especially as I was so tired all the time, and I did not at that time have the coeliac diagnosis to explain the fatigue.

I got an appointment fairly speedily with a cardiologist at Thiers, the cutlery centre. It's a town which always fills me with dread to visit because somehow, I always manage to take a wrong turning and find myself hopelessly lost up tiny narrow back streets on almost impossible gradients.

The town is built on the side of a hill alongside the river Durolle, the water having been essential in early times for grinding knife blades. Two-thirds of all the pocket knives, kitchen knives and table knives made in France are manufactured in Thiers, where the skills and craftsmanship date back more than six hundred years.

Because of my propensity for getting lost there, and my obsessive punctuality, I arrived in plenty of time to find a parking space and check that the cardiologist's consulting rooms really were where Google Maps and Via Michelin – well, as Michelin are head-quartered in Clermont-Ferrand, I have to support them, too – both said they were.

My brother and I had visited Thiers several times before he bought the Pink House. I managed to find my way to a car park we had used on a couple of occasions, which was handy for the centre of town. According to my intelligence, the cardiologist's place was on the main road up the big hill which snakes its way to the centre of town.

As I approached the address I was looking for, yet more evidence of the relaxed and laid-back attitude of the French to all matters health and safety. A large crane with a big wrecking ball was parked at the side of the main road, reducing the traffic to single lane, whilst it systemically bashed great lumps out of a building to demolish it.

Was the road closed? Was there a diversion in place? Were there *gendarmes* on the scene to control the traffic? Were there any safety officials of any description around to stop curious passers-by from getting too close to the proceedings? Of course not!

It was a busy Friday afternoon, with a steady flow of vehicles, good-naturedly negotiating their way through the ensuing bottle-neck. Passing pedestrians stopped for a glance, then carried on their way. Clearly demolishing a town-centre building in the middle of the day was a common occurrence in Thiers.

I had time for a little wander around, to go and *lécher les vitrines*, lick the windows, as the French call window shopping. My idea of window-licking was not to drool over the Louboutins but rather to gaze lustfully at the beautifully crafted knives. I love knives! In rural France it's quite normal for people, even seemingly respectable middle-aged ladies, to carry a pocket knife somewhere about their person. I probably have one in each bag I use frequently, from rucksack to daily use shoulder bag. It's not as sinister as it sounds. Many French love to peel their apples, so will often carry a knife to do so.

Then it was time to go and present myself at the cardiologist's and find out if my old ticker was still good for a few years.

The *cardiologue* was perhaps slightly younger than I, though not by much. As always, it was just him and me, no chaperone. He told me to take everything off except my knickers and to lie on the couch.

By now I was getting fairly used to stripping my kit off and, if not comfortable entirely, at least more relaxed. But one thing I don't like to take off is my socks, as I have possibly the coldest feet on the planet. I couldn't see how my little Cashmere ankle-socks were going to get in the way of diagnosing a possible heart condition but no, they too had to go, it seemed.

There was also none of the: 'Is it all right if I examine you?' stuff that's required in the UK before any doctor dare lay a finger on a patient. I was there to be examined so clearly the *cardiologue* was going to have to touch me.

The consulting room was two floors up in the old building, quite close to the one which was being demolished. There were no blinds or curtains or anything at the window, and there were buildings on the other side of the road with windows at the same height so anyone there could, theoretically, have seen me in all my glory. But it just seemed to be the accepted thing, so I went along with it.

The *cardiologue* listened to my heart and checked the pulse in both my lower legs. He then announced that he would do an ECG and told me to follow him. At this point I did start to feel a bit vulnerable in my state of undress as I trotted behind him across a corridor and into another room. I would certainly have preferred to have some socks on, at least. I could only hope that the next patients coming for a consultation were not about to appear in the same corridor, which might have been awkward. Although, then again, probably just routine, for the French.

Another trip across the corridor and into another room to examine something else then I could trot along in the *cardiologue's* wake to the first room to put my clothes back on, which felt something of a relief.

He said nothing particularly sinister had shown up and the murmur was indeed slight. But given the family history, he wanted to err on the side of caution so I went to reception and waited whilst a referral letter was prepared for me to go for a stress test, to have my heart monitored whilst I did active things. This would mean a trip into Clermont-Ferrand to the CHU, the university hospital, which had the facilities – the trip alone was certain to cause me plenty of stress.

I groaned inwardly at the prospect of driving into the city, which I hate. I'm quite happy to set off into the back of beyond in the country, but I just don't have the concentration these days for town driving. There is an excellent tram service around Clermont, with park and ride car parks. But I'm such a control freak I would be paranoid at the idea of being stranded away from my vehicle if anything went wrong with the tram. I dreaded being unable to get back to the van and get off home, where I always felt safest.

I'd arranged to meet my brother first on the outskirts of town on my way to CHU. He was recently back from a trip to UK and had come laden with gluten-free goodies for me, which were unavailable in France.

My brother gave me careful directions for the best way to get to the part of CHU which I needed to be in, since it is a large hospital over different sites, so I set off on my way, down the main road into the city.

As I approached the first of many traffic lights along my route, there was one of those impossible to make up coincidences. I found myself directly behind the exact same hearse which had carried my mother to the crematorium, the last time I had ventured into the city.

I found it more disturbing than I would have imagined. And

with my word association, it gave me an ear-worm of the
traditional song: 'Will the Circle Be Unbroken', which has the
verse and chorus:

> Well I told that undertaker
> Undertaker please drive slow
> For this lady you are carrying
> Lord, I hate to see her go
>
> Will the circle be unbroken
> By and by, Lord, by and by
> There's a better home a-waiting
> In the sky, Lord, in the sky

I was welling up, and it was becoming increasingly hard to
drive. Which is probably why I managed to sail through a red
light, to the extreme annoyance of a vehicle coming from my
left who should have had the right of way and signalled his
disapproval with a very long blast of his horn.

It was a huge relief when the hearse and I parted company
to go our separate ways, and I was able to compose myself
enough to get to CHU.

It was just as well that my heart murmur was slight and was
not greatly affecting me, as it was quite a hike from the large
car park to the building I needed to be in. An impressive thing I
noticed was that although the car park was so full that some of
us were having to park on a patch of waste ground next to it,
yet there were still rows of designated disabled parking spaces
left empty for those who truly needed them.

After a few false starts at finding the right set of stairs to
take me up to the part of the building where I needed to be, I
managed to find the right reception desk at which to present
my documents. French healthcare is not free and they don't
start to treat you until they've checked how payment will be
made. I'd always paid all my *cotisations*, social security

contributions, to entitle me to the precious *carte vitale*, health card, to show my entitlement. In addition I paid into a *mutuelle*, a top-up insurance scheme, to cover any shortfall between what the social security would pay and what the actual cost was.

They were running slightly late for my appointment so I sat outside the appointed room, hoping that the woman sitting next to me was not also due to have a stress test. Luckily, it turned out she was just there with the man who was already in, as when he emerged, they both left and it was my turn.

Once again it was a man conducting the tests, and as usual, I was alone with him in the room. I'd gone prepared in my skimpiest crop top, which was more like an itsy-bitsy, teeny-weeny bikini top, thinking it would be easy enough to stick the pads for the monitor around that. But no, it was once again a case of 'get 'em off' and get onto the treadmill wearing nothing but knickers and a lot of sticky pads wired up to a machine. I noticed that none of the pads was anywhere near the little crop top would have been so was forced to conclude that French men probably just liked looking at boobs at every available opportunity.

The stress test was nothing taxing at all, just walking briskly on the treadmill, under strict instructions to say something if I felt out of breath or had any chest pain at all. I didn't.

The test showed nothing abnormal. It seemed my heart would keep on trundling along for a bit longer yet, despite the murmur.

Chapter Twenty-one
Land of the Silver Birch

As any former Girl Guide or Boy Scout knows, 'Land of the Silver Birch' is a traditional Canadian folk song with words from a First Nations poem.

Land of the silver birch
Home of the beaver
Where still the mighty moose
Wanders at will

Blue lake and rocky shore
I will return once more
Boom diddy boom-boom, Boom diddy boom-boom
Boom diddy boom-boom boom

I've always loved silver birch trees, which have a special place in mythology and folklore. But I didn't have one growing on my land. Circumstances were going to arise causing me to change that.

One of the things about my grottage which I loved most was how quiet it was, sitting on the extreme southern edge of a very small hamlet. There was a one-bedroomed modern bungalow up the track opposite it, but its presence was not very evident because of my neighbour's apple and pear orchard in front of it. I also had a couple of big scrub willow trees on my '*potager*', kitchen garden, which was slowly starting to take shape, which mostly screened the bungalow from my view.

I'd been trying to combine outstanding jobs on the grottage into some sort of logical order to save doing things twice over. I had a large old cow byre underneath the hay loft which would make a perfect covered run for the dogs for when it was raining or too hot in the sun. But it probably hadn't been cleaned out in years so all the soil and old cow manure needed shovelling out by hand, as there was no way of getting a digger in there.

The residue from the floor was going to be liquid gold for growing fruit and vegetables, so needed hauling up the slope and across the road to the *potager*. Despite following a gluten-free diet to the point of paranoia, I was still tired and lacking in energy to do much of the work myself so I'd hired a young woman from Olliergues to make a start.

The grottage had been given a new roof shortly before I bought it and all the old roof tiles which had been removed were still stacked in the barn. Marie, my shoveller-in-chief, was using them, standing on their ends, to make edges for metre-square vegetable plots. Once the earth and manure from the cow byre had been lugged across there and tipped into them, this would effectively create raised beds, much easier for me to manage as I got older.

Being volcanic, the soil was incredibly fertile, even when it looked like not very much. I'd done some random test planting of root vegetables, just to see what would grow initially, not particularly thinking in terms of much of a crop. They all did very well, despite no tending at all, not even watering.

I'd planted carrots, potatoes and parsnips, which are one of my favourite vegetables and still something of a rarity in this part of France. They are slowly starting to appear, but I'd had a chuckle when a cookery programme on France Bleu radio had been doing a taste test for passers-by at a food fair using parsnips and hardly any of the people knew what they were or had ever eaten them.

There was a Saturday market in Olliergues every week, with a large fruit and veg stall, a van selling cheese, one selling meat, a woman selling eggs and home-made jams and an elderly woman selling a few home-grown vegetables, nuts and flowers. I liked her produce. The presence of live grubs in the leeks proved to me that they had not been drenched in pesticides.

The fruit and veg stall usually had a few parsnips, and I was buying some one day when an older lady looked on with interest and asked me if they were like a sort of turnip. I explained that they were sweeter and that my favourite way of eating them was oven roast and glazed with honey.

I completed my purchases and went on my way towards the library when the lady ran after me to check on the exact cooking instructions, saying she was going to get some for herself and her husband to try. I hope she enjoyed them as much as I did mine.

My *potager,* and the wild bit at the end where all the snakes lived, backed onto my neighbour's orchard, with the bungalow behind that and to the side of it, a big copse of trees. One day I heard the unmistakable insistent buzz of a chainsaw hard at work and to my dismay, I looked out of my window to see those trees systematically being cut down.

It turned out the land up there was being sold for a new house to be built. A young couple with two small children, whose family lived near St Loo and St Dongle, had wanted to build their house close to the family. For some reason, Olliergues' mayor had opposed the build, but had instead agreed for it to take place opposite the grottage.

I'd always planned on planting fruits trees on part of the plot of land to make a *verger*, an orchard, and it looked as if this was giving me just the nudge I needed to get on and get it done. But now as well as the fruit trees, I was going to need to plant something bigger to screen the new house, which would sit high up looking down towards my grottage.

There was a local small nursery which sold plants, shrubs, trees and so on. I'd made a good start on creating a garden and had already bought a lot of plants from the owner, Bruno, who was very nice and very knowledgeable. I arranged for him to come and quote for some native trees and shrubs for a bit of screening, as well as some heritage varieties of fruit trees - apples, pears and plums.

The view from the middle section of my plot of land, where the trees would go, was superb, with an uninterrupted line of sight to the Puy de Dôme volcano, flanked by its chain of lesser peaks to the west. I had already decided that it was where I wanted my ashes to be scattered, and with that in mind, I got Bruno to plant a silver birch, right where my ashes would go.

There's no problem in France about having ashes scattered on your own property. The only thing you're not allowed to do is keep someone's ashes sitting in the house for ever more. As it's a secular country, there's no requirement for any form of religious ceremony or consecrated ground.

As I have no children, anything I possess, which is very little, would go to Mother's two favourite carers. And as I have always presumed I will outlive my brother, they have instructions on what to do with my mortal remains and any remaining animals I might have when the time comes. But I wanted to make sure there was no financial burden on them at all in doing so, so it was time to sort myself out a funeral plan, to make sure everything was paid for up front.

Augerolles has a small funeral director, so I phoned them first and asked to go along and discuss things, as I always prefer to shop small and local, whenever I can.

Who would have thought a couple of hours planning one's own funeral could be such fun! But the funeral director was so nice and helpful, and we chatted about all sorts of topics including funerals, that it was an enjoyable afternoon.

I started off with a tricky question for him, as I wanted a cardboard coffin. Just as Mother had been, I was vehemently opposed to the idea of a using beautiful and expensive piece of wood in which I would reside for a very short period of time, which would then be destroyed by fire. It was not just the cost, it was the whole concept of the waste I disliked.

The undertaker said he didn't think cardboard coffins were yet accepted in many parts of France, although I had found a firm in France which was selling them, or rather, ones made of cellulose. But he was extremely helpful and telephoned the crematorium to check for me. They confirmed that there were still some issues preventing them from being permitted at the present time.

I settled on the plainest, least expensive wooden coffin on the books, and had the undertaker write into the agreement that should a cardboard or cellulose one become permissible at a future date, that would be substituted at the time and the cost of the funeral plan adjusted accordingly.

Next came the choice of songs to be played at the funeral. Absolutely no religious schmaltz for me. I was having Buffy Sainte Marie singing 'Up Where We Belong', Sandy Denny singing 'Who Knows Where the Time Goes' and Eva Cassidy singing 'Fields of Gold'.

Lots of friends thought it incredibly morbid to be planning funerals, and also somehow to be tempting fate. But I'm nothing if not practical; I like planning and sorting out arrangements, and have a horror of nobody knowing what to do in a certain set of circumstances. Now everything was in place and all paid for, I could relax and enjoy what I hoped would be many years in my grottage.

Bruno and his co-worker came on a cold and snowy day to plant the trees. The young silver birch was delightful and I hoped I would see it grow up tall and strong before being sprinkled round its roots as fertiliser.

One of the hot debates between the French and the English is over who grows the best roses, with each nation claiming that honour. I'd always wanted to grow a Kiftsgate rose, one of the biggest and most vigorous rambling roses there is, capable of reaching ten metres in both height and spread. The new build opposite gave me the perfect opportunity to do so.

Planted alongside one of the big oak pillars for the iron gates, with training, it could swarm along the top of the fence and run riot up the hazel tree in the corner, hopefully providing an effective and fragrant screen between my garden and the view of the new house, which was going to be a big one.

For me, no plant is worth growing unless it either provides food for bees and other beneficial insects, or has a beautiful fragrance. Which is why I love old fashioned roses with their heady musk scent, oriental lilies you can smell from yards away, honeysuckle, mock orange blossom and, of course, the lovely broad leaved limes, with their incredibly sweet fragrance.

I'd now made a perennial flower border down the long side of the garden and planted shrubs alongside the fence at the top, firethorn, buddleia, lilac and viburnum. Once they grew taller, they would help to support the weight of the big Kiftsgate rose.

You couldn't call the grassed area a lawn, as such, as I left great swathes of it uncut for the bees and other pollinators. But I did try to keep it mown round the edges, to show off the flowers to full advantage, and on the area where the dogs liked to play. One of the problems with gardening organically and trying to welcome all wildlife is that some of it is more desirable than others. There was a huge problem with ticks in the area, spread by the deer and the wild boar.

For some reason Ci was a total tick magnet. After every walk I would have to pick at least a dozen off him, and was constantly finding more, partly engorged with blood, all over him. Fleur picked up far fewer, although she did get some. Typically Ci was the one who hated being handled and hated having them removed, whereas Fleur was much more stoic about it.

Natural remedies? Essential oils? I could write a whole

book about them! I'd tried just about everything anyone had recommended, including the 'this never fails' remedies. Clearly Auvergnat ticks like a challenge. I would even find them on myself after walks in the woods, and often in the most intimate of places.

I knew that some of the proprietary pipettes from the vet were effective. I also knew they were controversial regarding their effects on bees and other insects so I was loath to use them. On the other hand, I didn't want to risk my dogs' health. Reluctantly, I bought some of the chemical collars.

Not long afterwards, Fleur was extremely lame when she woke up one morning, and there was nothing to see or feel to explain it. I don't like symptoms without logical explanation, so I decided to take her to the vet.

My vet, in nearby Courpière, was delightful; it was always a pleasure to go for the long chats we would have. He was also a very good vet. He examined her carefully, then asked if she had had any other symptoms, especially any yellowish diarrhoea. She hadn't, but he said he had already seen two dogs that same morning, presenting with sudden lameness, which turned out to be piroplasmosis, a tick-borne disease, and asked if she could have been bitten by a tick. Certainly she could.

He decided to treat her for the disease as a precaution, as he said the treatment would do no harm even if it proved unnecessary. When I stopped to give both dogs a short walk on our way home, Fleur obligingly confirmed his provisional diagnosis with the yellow diarrhoea.

So I optimistically continued to mow part of the grass to keep it close cropped, although the woods continued to be crawling with ticks. Very reluctantly, I also started a regime of using the tick repellents bought from the vet.

Now that the house and grounds were starting to take shape, I could celebrate with a few more visits from friends. Any excuse to throw a tea-party! But I also wanted to invite some of my friends over to do 'ladies wot lunch.'

Chapter Twenty-two
Be Prepared

Entertaining at the grottage was always going to be difficult, unless the weather was kind. The sitting room was small and very narrow, just room for a sofa, the television and a small table to seat two people.

The kitchen was much larger but I had made it my work station. I paid a local carpenter to create me a gorgeous half glazed stable door out of sustainable local oak, with double glazed panels in the top section. Whenever it was warm enough, I had the doors open so the dogs could come and go and I could look out on the garden and fields.

When it was cold, I was close enough to Kevin the Kitchen Range to keep nice and warm, and I could still see out of the window and the top door. I need constant contact with the outdoors.

With my big mahogany work desk, a small sideboard and the kitchen units, there was no room for anyone to sit and eat, except me when I was on my own. Then I could perch on a stool and use one of the tiled work surfaces as a table.

But for guests, the ideal was for the weather to be kind so we could all sit outside in the sunshine on the deck, with plenty of room to spread out.

I wanted to invite my former English conversation group students to come and visit, to see what I had done with the place, as they had been hearing horror stories of it ever since I first decided to buy it. I was still in touch with several of them and as two of them in particular were keen gardeners, they promised to come armed with plants and cuttings from their own gardens to help me get mine started.

The weather had some surprises in store for us, though, in the form of a violent storm which knocked out the electricity the day before their visit. Luckily, I had the gas cooker to bake cakes and scones so I wasn't too worried, just optimistically hoping that the day of their visit would be fine enough to sit outside.

No such luck! Howling wind, torrential rain and still no electricity. The Massif Central at its capricious best. There was nothing for it but to bring garden chairs into the small sitting room and do the best I could to welcome my visitors.

There was still no electricity and, with the heavy rain, it was dark inside. Luckily I had the little solar panels which would run two quite bright lights for long enough for us to have afternoon tea in a decent amount of light.

For economy, I hadn't gone for a separate landline telephone, I just had the phone via internet. So of course, no electricity meant no internet and therefore no phone. My visitors all had my mobile number but the signal was non-existent indoors and the weather was not conducive to scampering about in the garden trying to get enough bars to send text messages. Confusingly, the phone would often receive texts when showing no signal, but sending was quite another matter.

Hopefully my visitors would find the grottage without too many problems as it's not easy to locate on a first visit. GPS is not much use either, since it often denies the existence of my address altogether and when it does accept it, it usually sends poor unwary travellers up a very difficult route with a sharp bend bordering on a hairpin.

What I didn't know was that the strong winds had also brought down some trees on the road so my poor visitors were having to cope with finding alternative routes. Luckily there are several ways to get to the grottage, but none of them easy.

My older ladies arrived first and I rushed out to meet them, armed with large golf umbrellas to bring them inside with as much protection from the torrential rain as possible. True to their word, they had brought pots and pots of wonderful plants and cuttings for me, all perfect cottage garden plants. They'd remembered my preferred colour scheme of blue, too, the most attractive colour for bees. There were delphiniums and catmint, lupins and Canterbury bells, and all sorts of wonderful fragrant herbs like hyssop and borage.

Next came my two teenage students, the sisters, with their mother to drive them, also armed with gifts of plants. I was spoiled, and going to have such fun planning where to plant them all.

There was just enough of a window in the weather for me to show them round the grounds and outbuildings before the downpour started again so we had to pile into the tiny sitting room for our afternoon tea. My visitors were all duly impressed with the efficiency of my little solar lighting kits, especially given the recent bad weather and lack of any sunshine. Despite the difficulties, we had a good time. It was wonderful to catch up with friends and a chance for all of them to practise their English on me.

Next on my busy social agenda was to host a luncheon for some of my new ex-pat friends. I hadn't specifically set out to enlarge my circle of non-French friends, but Christine had introduced me to two friends of hers, Linda and Muta, and we made a point of getting together occasionally for a meal and a good old natter.

Christine had of course seen the grottage many times, from before I bought it to its current state of habitable but still lacking some finishing touches. Definitely shabby chic. The other two had not yet been.

The weather forecast was not brilliant for the day of the

luncheon but, channelling my inner Baden Powell once more, I assured the ladies we would be lunching outdoors, even if it had to be in one of my tents.

I really enjoy cooking, and now I was starting to get to grips with managing without gluten, I was getting a bit more adventurous in what I prepared. I spent ages planning a menu that would be enjoyable but not too taxing. Above all, knowing by now the havoc the Auvergnat weather could wreak with the carefully laid plans of mice and men, I chose something which could mostly be prepared in advance or easily finished off with the bottled gas cooker if the electricity failed.

After much deliberation, I settled on a starter of *blini* with smoked salmon and cream cheese, a main of hummus with spicy flatbreads, tabbouleh made with quinoa, since I could no longer eat bulgur wheat, poached salmon, and hippy spinach and mushroom quiche cups.

Blini were fine, as they could be made entirely from buckwheat which, being a primitive grain, contains no gluten. The flatbreads I could make from a gluten-free flour blend my brother had brought back for me from the UK.

Pudding would be a chocolate almond cake cooked in a ring mould with the centre filled with fresh strawberries, and a non-alcoholic lemon syllabub in little glass pots to go with it.

The hippy spinach was a joke I was playing on my unsuspecting guests. It was actually fresh young nettles, and I was curious to know if anyone would identify them. The quiche cups were a clever idea I had seen for a gluten-free quiche. There was no pastry, the egg mix was simply poured into silicone muffin moulds and cooked that way.

In case Mother Nature had plans for us on the weather front, I put up the Quechua Base tent. It fitted perfectly onto the deck which had the advantage of being flat, as none of the garden was flat enough to create a tented dining area. It was easy enough to secure the guy ropes to the deck in case of strong winds. There was plenty of room inside for a table, four chairs and even a little side table.

Now all I had to do was await my guests. Christine was, as usual, punctual. What I didn't know was that both Linda and Muta regularly made an art form of getting spectacularly lost and arriving very late to their destination.

I'd given them very careful directions of how to find the best route and told them on no account to trust the GPS. Because they were chatting, they missed the turn-off for Augerolles and went sailing on down the Dore valley towards Olliergues. Beautiful scenery and a lovely road, in good condition, but not the most direct route to the grottage.

Of course when they tried to phone my mobile for further directions, both they and I were experiencing signal problems in a notorious black-spot for most of the major phone networks in France. I was rushing up and down the garden, valiantly waving my little mobile in the air in search of a signal, whilst theirs kept cutting out.

But eventually we managed to communicate and soon we saw them sailing past the grottage having totally failed to spot it. How anyone can fail to notice my distinctive bright yellow van covered all over in hippy stickers remains a mystery. They did however spot me as I raced out into the road behind them, jumping up and down and waving, especially as I was wearing what Christine rather unkindly called my romper suit, which is in fact my very comfy bright yellow denim dungarees.

At last we were all sitting down to the table, after I'd given my new visitors a quick tour of my little grottage.

Linda was extremely taken with my choice of tent. When I'd told them we would definitely be outside, in a tent if necessary, she had somehow imagined we would be crouched on the ground in a tiny little two-man backpacker type of affair. She was most impressed with the height and space of Count Basie. One of its very good points is that if you need to close up the sides against the weather, you can open up good-sized mesh half-moon windows in the top of three sides for light and ventilation.

For some reason my guests had also thought that lunch was going to be a limp egg and cress sandwich, in old hiking and camping tradition, eaten whilst squatting in said small tent. So the sit-down luncheon in the roomy expanse of the Base was a pleasant surprise.

Since neither Christine nor I drink alcohol, she from choice, me of necessity, she had kindly brought a locally made sparkling peach wine for us and I had plenty of grape juice. It was a most enjoyable afternoon. The tent added a wonderfully quirky character to the meal and was a boon whenever there was a sprinkling or rain or a bit of a chilly breeze blowing.

For me it was great fun to be back in a tent again. So much so that I decided to leave it out on the deck and sleep in it for a couple of nights.

With so much work to do on the grottage, I hadn't been going away on my little camping trips quite so much and I missed them. For the second anniversary of Mother's death, I'd had a couple of days away in a chalet, not all that far away, up in the Haut Livradois, simply because I couldn't find a site open for tent camping in March.

Although the site was quite close to the edge of the small town, the chalet I was allocated was high up towards the back of the site with good access directly to woods and footpaths, and with a nice view down over the town and to the woods beyond.

It was quiet, being early in the season, and not many of the chalets were occupied. When the dogs started looking through the glass door and barking in the direction of the next chalet, I assumed we were to have neighbours in there. I looked out of the window and saw who the neighbours were. Two small grey and white rabbits were sitting happily in front of the chalet, quite unconcerned, nibbling the grass. They were clearly domestic, not wild, and seemed to have free run of the site, as the dogs and I encountered them randomly around the place during our stay, and there were bowls of food and water left out for them.

I loved being at my grottage. But I also loved my little trips away. Time to start planning some more, and with more visitors to come, I had the perfect excuse.

Chapter Twenty-three
Silly Tart

As a child, I don't remember being as clumsy as I have become with advancing years. But I'm certainly making up for lost time.

I've had accidents it shouldn't be possible to have, and certainly ones which no-one believes when you tell them. On one memorable occasion, when I had a small-holding in Wales, I had to take a week off work from my job as a reporter on the local newspaper as I got concussion when a goat fell on my head. No, I don't think my editor believed me either, but it was true.

The neck injury I received from a horse called George and which has plagued me for more than thirty years was from a fluke head butt which did so much damage I had difficulty convincing the hospital's Accident and Emergency service I really had done it without falling off.

Despite all my efforts, I always managed to inflict some sort of harm on myself. I would carefully don oven-proof gloves to fill Kevin the Kitchen Range up with fuel without burning my hands. Then I'd lean forward to open the door and catch the tip of my nose on the hotplate. And of course no-one but a complete idiot would try to check if something was bubbling away in the oven by leaning closer, with their ear just above the hob. Would they? Silly tart!

But there couldn't possibly be any danger at all in packing

up to go away for a few days in the Cantal with best friend Jill. Could there?

As ever, I'd been greatly looking forward to Jill's visit and had planned to take her down to the chalet site in the Cantal where the ice cream was so good. I'd booked one of the colourful hippy chalets, down at the bottom of the track, and we were going to drive down the day after her arrival.

Her flight into Clermont-Ferrand from Southampton (the real one, of course, not Cunlhat!) was on time, and touched down on a lovely July day. The Auvergne was looking its beautiful best, bathed in sunshine, hot, but not uncomfortably so.

We would be taking my small camping trailer with us so we didn't have to overload the back of the van. The dogs travelled in an airy cage and there was now a roof ventilator I'd had installed, but with too much luggage squashed around the cage, it risked being too hot for them on the journey.

We were having a leisurely start on the day of our departure. Breakfast on the deck, followed by a short leg stretch for the dogs, then finishing off packing all we would need for a few days away. The cats would be confined to the barn in our absence, to keep them safe, with plenty of food and water to see them through. Christine would pop over to check on them, take in the post and generally make sure that all was well.

We were almost ready for the off. I was just putting the finishing touches to a picnic lunch to have on the journey which included the essential flask of boiling water to make tea. I have two good stainless steel flasks, elderly and battered now, much as I am. They are the clever sort with a button in the stopper so you don't even need to unscrew the stopper to pour, just depress the button. One had become a little tricky with age but I still considered it serviceable.

I was carrying what my Luxembourg granny called a lazy man's load and always advised me against carrying. In other words my hands and arms were rather more full than they should have been. One flask was carried from my shoulder by its strap, the other was tucked into the crook of my left elbow.

The side gate from the garden to the parking area where Roo the Kangoo awaited departure had a rather awkward catch which sometimes involved lifting the gate ever so slightly with one foot whilst wriggling the bolt to get it to slide.

There followed one of those moments when brain and limbs were taking rather a long time to communicate with one another for some reason. My left hand was hurting, rather a lot. Unfortunately, my brain was taking an unacceptably long time to register the appeal for help.

When I looked down, I could see that the stopper of the flask under my left arm had come loose and was pouring a slow but steady stream of just-boiled water over the back of my hand. And I had rather a lot of things to put down before I could do anything about righting it.

My dogs come first in my life, always and unconditionally. I put the flask somewhere they could not knock it over and hurt themselves, then secured the gate before hurrying into the kitchen and heading straight for the cold tap.

My hand by now was screaming at me and for the moment I was having trouble saying anything other than 'ouch' to explain to Jill what was going on. The fleshy part between my thumb and forefinger seemed to have caught the worst of it, but there was a lot of redness everywhere and most of it hurt.

Jill and I are both first aiders so knew the best and only thing to do was to leave it under running cold water for as long as possible. But at some point I was going to need to get in the van for the fairly long drive down to the Cantal.

We decided in the end the best way would be to put ice packs over the burn, with gauze underneath to prevent them from delivering burns of their own. I had some squishy ones with gel inside which I thought would fit the bill and we could put spares in the cool box we were taking with us. I would also stop at the *pharmacie* in Olliergues before we set off on our journey.

The burn was very red and just starting to pucker around the edges. The pharmacist gave me some cooling gel to apply and said if it didn't improve, I would need to visit a doctor. He also suggested *Doliprane* for the pain. *Doliprane* is paracetamol and is the French go-to for any and every ailment.

We had a pleasant drive, with several stops on the way to stretch our legs and let the dogs stretch theirs. Whenever we had a cup of tea, I was more than happy to let Jill pour the boiling water. I wasn't keen on a repeat episode.

The day was growing hotter and as we drove, the sun was constantly beating down on my hands on the steering wheel, which was increasing the intensity of the pain. Jill kindly poured cold water over the hand as I drove and kept renewing the soaked gauze and changing the ice packs, as by now the heat from the burn was melting them quickly.

By the time we arrived safely at our destination and I went into reception to discover which of the chalets we had been allocated, my hand was very painful and a large blister was starting to form.

I asked if they could spare me some more ice, since all of the ice packs had now melted. I uncovered the hand and Alain, the owner, exclaimed, '*ah la vache!*', rather like 'blimey!' at the sight of it. He and his wife Ghislaine were most solicitous and full of advice intended to be helpful. They were all for piercing the blister and treating it with essential oils, another great French favourite. Only it was MY poorly paw, it hurt a lot and I did not feel like letting anyone near it. I strongly suspected I might be tempted to bite them if they tried. Especially anyone armed with a needle!

I thanked them kindly for the ice, assured them it would be fine as I always heal very quickly, then Ghislaine took us down the track and let us choose the chalet we wanted, as they weren't many residents.

We opted for the funky yellow and magenta one which had the best view. Inside it was basic but functional, with everything we could possibly need. There was one double bedroom, which I suggested would be good for Jill, a twin-bedded room, and a double *clic-clac* bed in the main living room. There was a shower and a separate loo, but just the kitchen sink, no separate wash hand basin. There was also a gas cooker, a microwave, a coffee maker and a gas wall heater if the evenings got cool, as we were at the highest village in the Cantal.

It was perfect for our needs. I decided to take the *clic-clac*, as the French call them. It's a sofa which, with a click and a clack, opens out into a double bed. Surprisingly comfortable and ideal for me and a couple of lazy collie dogs.

The next day we were going to be entertaining at the chalet. I'd met Tom and Chrissie through Facebook and grown to think of them as good friends, although we had not yet met. One day their incredible story will be a book in its own right, undoubtedly a best seller, so I won't give too much away. Suffice it to say that, despite taking the greatest possible care and doing everything by the book, when they bought their new home in the Cantal, they found themselves saddled with not one but two sitting tenants about whom they knew nothing.

Despite fighting battles in various French courts they were still unable to dislodge either of them. This prevented them from carrying out the essential works to adapt the property to their particular health needs, which effectively meant they would never be able to live in it.

They'd had instead to take to the road, house and pet sitting when they could, living in a tent when they couldn't – Hobos in France, as they called themselves.

It was about an hour and a half's drive for them to come to the chalet and they left in plenty of time. As I discovered later, Chrissie is not a great traveller, so they tend to drive slowly. I had a cheery text from them saying they had stopped for a coffee in nearby Condat and would be with us within the half-hour.

Tom's health issues meant he needed to try to follow a gluten-free diet too but he was not convinced he would like it. I'd therefore prepared things like quinoa tabbouleh and hummus with gluten-free cumin seed flat-breads for him to try. I'd made the flat-bread dough in advance and brought it with us. It simply needed shaping and flattening then cooking on the electric *plancha* I'd brought with us, not knowing if there would be anything suitable available.

The trouble was, the blister on my hand had now taken on the proportions of an extra from the film 'Alien' and looked as if some strange creature was about to burst forth from its watery insides. There was no way I could handle dough, certainly not one-handed.

Luckily Jill stepped up to the plate as sous-chef and sorted things out. Meanwhile we waited for our guests to arrive. And waited. And waited.

I was surprised as, knowing Tom was an ex naval officer, I'd rather imagined they would be punctual. But I'd forgotten the vagaries of the Auvergnat weather. We'd had a bit of a storm earlier on and thought no more about it. A plaintive text from Chrissie informed us their most direct route was now blocked by hailstones as big as marbles causing havoc on the road, so they were having to divert to the longer route.

Finally the poor weary travellers arrived. Tom and Chrissie were every bit as lovely in the flesh as on social media and we had a wonderful time. In deference to our visitors, not wanting to put them off their food, I had covered up my increasingly obscene-looking blister with a light gauze dressing.

Tom asked what I had done so I said it was blistered from a burn. He started talking about a blistered foot he'd had one time from new boots. I couldn't resist it. Saying: 'No, **this** is a blister,' I revealed The Alien in all its glory. Tom had the grace to look impressed.

The next day the blister was even bigger and the feeling of pressure on my skin was most unpleasant. I decided I had better see a doctor after all. We changed our nature reserve visiting plans for the day, instead heading to the nearby small town of Marcenat. Jill stayed with the van to make sure the dogs were cool enough whilst I went first to the *pharmacie* for advice.

Once again, when I revealed The Alien, I was treated to an '*ah la vache*!'. The pharmacist said it certainly needed to be looked at by a doctor. He said the good news was that there was one in town, just up the road, who was consulting that same day.

Many French doctors still have small surgeries with no receptionist, often in the ground floor of their own house, or in one in which they rent rooms. This particular doctor consulted on the ground floor of the old *gendarmerie* building. When I went into the waiting room, there was absolutely no sign of anyone and no sound from any of the adjoining rooms.

Eventually a man came in, carrying a newspaper and some shopping. He, it turned out, was the doctor. As no-one else was waiting, he ushered me straight into his surgery and I unveiled The Alien once more. This time it was greeted with a '*putain*!'

It was, the doctor told me, a second degree burn. It needed to be lanced and debrided, the dead skin cut away, and would require daily dressing initially, reducing to once every two days until it was healed.

When I replied to his question about my work, saying that I used a computer, he offered me a sick note for a week, much to my surprise. He advised *Doliprane* for the pain when necessary, and wrote me a prescription for disinfectant and all the dressings I would need. He also wrote me a prescription for a nurse to come to the house to do the dressings. Amazing. I simply could not imagine the UK health service providing all of that for what was, after all, a self-inflicted burn.

The relief when he lanced it was blissful and instantaneous.

He deftly cleaned it up and dressed it for me and I went on my way feeling almost normal once more.

It meant Jill and I could enjoy the rest of our visit, with trips to the nature reserve, walks in the hills and relaxing with our books on the little patio in front of our funky chalet. From there we could watch the cattle up on the *estives* wandering slowly along the skyline in Indian file, presumably going off for a drink.

Once back home, I didn't take advantage of my sick note to claim a week off work. It seemed to me a bit of overkill for a small burn. I was still anxious not to draw any kind of attention to myself as a possible scrounger, before I got the results of my frogification application. I did, however, set up the nurse visits to do the dressings on the burn at my home. With the dead layers of skin removed, it was a bit like a piece of raw meat and I was anxious to avoid infection. Luckily it was already starting to heal with the customary speed of my normally fast metabolism.

Another impressive display of French healthcare at its best. Sadly, in comparison, French customer care is still in its infancy, as I was about to find out.

Chapter Twenty-four
Customer Service

After-sales care and customer service in France are legendary – and not in a good way. They range from non-existent, via rude and condescending up to, if you are lucky, quite good.

To date, my experiences had been quite good. Sometimes, inevitably, it depends on how people approach the problem, as you often get back what you give out, and that goes double for attitude.

People who remain calm, quiet and polite are often, though not always, met with the same level of courtesy. I had on occasion had to take things back to bigger stores like Carrefour for exchange and had not run into any problems.

Then there was the memorable occasion at the small Champion supermarket in Combronde, when I lived at the Pink House, where I had taken my old van for a clean with the jet wash. I put my two euro coin in the slot, wash lance in hand, and prepared to do battle with the mud.

Instead, the hose split in several places at once and I was covered pretty much all over in hot water and foam. Since there is a limit to how wet a person can actually get, and I reached it pretty much instantaneously, I decided I might as well continue and do the best I could. In any case, I needed to use the rinse cycle to clean all the foam off myself but, since that was cold and it was a chilly morning, I didn't enjoy that part much at all.

I then splashed and squelched my way over to the store and

went just inside the door. I flagged down the first passing member of staff I saw and asked them to bring the manager to me. I waited, dripping constantly, with a large puddle forming round my feet.

The manager, a pleasant young man who knew me by sight, was utterly mortified when he saw the state of me and heard what had happened. He couldn't have apologised any more sincerely. He immediately handed me a ten euro shopping voucher, refunded the cost of the wash and asked me to send him the dry cleaning bills for my clothes plus details of anything which was damaged beyond repair. He was not very reassuring when he pointed out that the soap mixture was quite caustic and seemed relieved I had at least rinsed myself off. He also assured me he would immediately label the jet wash out of order, to prevent further incident.

It has to be said that I don't have much luck with jet washes. I had an interesting encounter with one in Courpière, the nearest town to the grottage, but that was a case of me being a silly tart yet again, not a malfunction. I put my two euro piece in the slot and started washing Roo the Kangoo, but it was dirtier than I thought. I was going to need to put another coin in the slot when the first one ran out.

Of course, only a very silly tart would think that putting the lance on the floor whilst going to the machine and adding more money was a good idea. That particular lance did not have any lever to squeeze to start it squirting water, which it immediately began to do as soon as I dropped the second coin in the slot. That in turn led to the hose and lance writhing round the floor like a big snake in its death throes, soaking me and whacking my shins, whilst I made valiant attempts to leap on it and wrestle it into submission. Thank goodness there were no other customers about that morning to witness my antics.

But back to customer services. It's probably Murphy's Law which dictates that the most trouble I was to experience with after sales service would be with two of the most expensive investments I made for the grottage.

The all-singing all-dancing *micro-station d'épuration*, mini-sewage treatment plant, had so far been doing its business with my business, so to speak, without fault. The hum of the air pump was a little annoying but I was slowly getting used to it and it no longer troubled me at night. I may just have been getting harder of hearing, of course. There was absolutely no odour and everything seemed to be working very well. I paid for an annual service, as that was something I didn't fancy doing myself, and all appeared to fine.

The spring of 2013 was a wet one, followed by a hot, dry spell. I didn't think much about it, or consider if it would pose any problems. One July day, a sudden insistent beeping brought me out to the garden to look in the control box where the pump was. The audible alarm was going off, and when I looked inside, the alarm lights were showing there was a problem with the air flow to the pump.

I switched the pump off to silence the alarm and went in search of the instruction manual to find out what to do. Phone the manufacturer, it said, which is what I did. They told me sometimes the alarm could sound for no real reason so to leave it switched off for a while then try resetting it.

This I did and the pump purred into action like a contented cat once more, with no sound of the alarm going off. Until twenty-four hours later, when it went off again. The same thing happened on three consecutive days, so I called their customer service department.

They said they would arrange for one of their engineers to call as soon as one was available. Meantime I should leave the pump switched off and not to worry as the unit was designed to be perfectly safe for up to two weeks without the pump running, in case of breakdown.

True to their word, they phoned me back with an appointment in two weeks' time. It unfortunately fell on a day when Jill and I would be on our little jaunt down to the Cantal.

They said there was no need for me to be present, just to consent to their engineer entering the garden in my absence to fix the problem, which I gladly did. I also hastened to assure them that the signs about Beware of the Dogs would not apply as the dogs would be on holiday with me.

When Jill and I arrived back, there was no familiar reassuring hum coming from the air pump. It was still switched off, and my note of explanation about the fault was still inside the box which housed the pump.

Once we got inside and I got the Internet back up and running, there were three missed telephone calls from the engineer, confirming his imminent visit, which was strange. Considering I had told the firm I would not be there, it seemed pointless for him to be ringing my home telephone.

When I sorted through the post Christine had brought in from the letterbox on her cat-feeding visits, I found a note from the engineer saying he had called as planned but as there was no-one at home, he had gone away again.

Not best pleased, I phoned the firm to ask why my message had not been passed on to the man on the ground and when I could expect a return visit. It was then I discovered that the firm, which was based in Toulouse, more than four hundred and fifty kilometres away, did not have any service technicians in the Auvergne. One had been sent out specially and would not now be back in the area for a few more weeks. Wonderful after sales service!

It's lucky I have so many free phone calls with my internet package. I probably used them all up phoning the manufacturers for a new date. In the end the boss of the company himself phoned me one evening, full of apology. It was, he said, a problem many people had been experiencing, caused by the weather. The hot spell after all the rain was causing a build-up of condensation in the air pipes of the units. It made sense.

It was to be a full eight weeks from breakdown date until

my unit was fixed and working once more. To be fair, there was no odour problem at all during that time, but I was relieved to have it functioning correctly once more. The formerly annoying hum of the pump now became a welcome sound.

For some time I had been considering getting photo-voltaic panels for the grottage roof. As it was largely south-facing, it should generate a reasonable amount of electricity to sell back to the electricity company. My own electricity bills were fairly modest. The economies I made by using my small camping solar kits for lighting and favouring the rocket stoves, or even my high-speed camping gas cooker over the electric kettle, paid off.

There was currently a huge push to sell PV panels to householders in France and hardly a week went by when I didn't get at least one cold call trying to sell me some. I hadn't bothered to block cold calls as they were a good opportunity for spontaneous French practice.

One evening I received one in English. Not very brilliant English, and the man was heartily relieved when I said I was quite happy to speak French. He told me he'd taken a guess, based on my name, that I was English, so thought he would try in that language. I admired his enterprise, so I listened to his *spiel*. I'm not usually swayed by such things, having done hard selling myself as a chugger (charity mugger – the people who verbally mug you in the name of charity in the streets and outside shops) but I found myself agreeing to let one of their sales representatives call.

The salesman who called must really have had a silver tongue because, having been absolutely determined not to, I found myself signing up to a deal to borrow what seemed like a horrendous amount of money for the installation of the panels. At least there was nothing to pay up front, and if the salesman's figures were to be trusted, the amount of electricity I would be able to sell back to EDF should cover the cost of the loan. Once it was paid off, of course, the money earned would be mine. Worst case scenario, I had some meagre savings to cover the loan, and as bank interest was currently at an all-time low, it could well be better use of capital.

Amazingly, an appointment was made in less than two weeks' time for the installation of the panels. The company I had picked seemed very good. They had an impressive website and glossy brochures. As it's my line of work, I knew they were good quality and not cheap.

When their fitters arrived, it was three men in a rather scruffy and battered old van, with no company logo or anything. The men were Romanian, as it turned out, of whom only one spoke any French. They seem to work quickly and efficiently, stripping off roof tiles and stacking them neatly where I instructed. In no time at all, my roof was sporting twelve photovoltaic panels.

The French-speaker was the electrician and he installed the meters in the kitchen, which would soon, hopefully, show me how much money the panels were earning for me. He also put in the transformers, which had to go inside the barn.

The salesman had made various comments on where the meters, transformers and so on could be installed, but the Romanian electrician was having none of it. There was much teeth-sucking and head shaking before he selected the best place in his opinion.

I figured it was like hairdressers who always like to tut and sigh and ask: 'Who cut your hair last?' I was once delighted to be able to say, with perfect honesty, to a hairdresser who asked that question that it had been he himself who had cut mine last.

Now everything was installed on my property. The next step would be for EDF to come and do something to the meter boxes outside in the road to install the correct things for the electricity I was generating to be fed back into the grid. Note my impressive use of technical terms.

As it was the solar panel installers who were paying for this, I had to wait for them to pay EDF before they would even issue an appointment to come and do the next stage of the installation. It was the beginning of April, so with the sunniest months of the year ahead of us, I was itching to get the costly panels working and starting to earn their keep.

Some people think that France is hot and sunny all year round, all over. The UK government clearly do, since they stopped the winter fuel allowances to UK pensioners living in France. The truth is, in the Massif Central, you can get almost any sort of weather at any time of year. In August, we had a colossal storm with absolutely torrential rain which, most unusually, was blowing up from due south.

It was extremely violent, but mercifully only short-lived, so I thought no more about it, until I heard the sound of water dripping. There was water leaking through the kitchen ceiling, splashing onto Kevin the Kitchen Range and, more alarmingly, trickling down the light-fitting in the centre of the room.

The kitchen is partly under the shower room, which was where the water appeared to be coming from, so I rushed upstairs expecting to find a burst pipe, or a forgotten tap left running. Instead there was water running down the partition wall in the shower room, clearly coming from the loft.

I pulled the loft ladder down and went up, switching on the light, and also armed with a torch for peering into any dark corners. I was just hoping that the water tank had not sprung a leak. Instead I could see, from the pools of water on the floor, that my previously new and watertight roof was leaking like the proverbial sieve, since the installation of the solar panels.

It was the first time since their installation that we had had a storm from the south, in itself a rare occurrence, and it had clearly found some weakness in the installation somewhere.

I got straight on the phone to the installers, not best pleased, and they promised to have someone round three days later to put things right. I took photographs of all the leaks, and carefully covered all my stored items in the attic with a large tarpaulin to protect them from any further ingress of water.

Another battered old van, another Romanian roofing team, just two, this time. It was a cold and damp day and, to be fair to them, they stayed up on the roof a long time. Once again, only one spoke French. He said he couldn't really see any reason for the sudden leak but agreed that it was clearly linked to the installation.

His best guess was that roofing nails had been replaced without backing washers, and with the driving rain from the south, rain had found its way into the tiniest of cracks. He and his team-mate lifted all the nails, put washers behind them, and sealed everything sealable with mastic. I would only truly know if they had been successful with the next southerly storm, but as they were a rarity, it could be some time.

EDF had still not been to do whatever it was they needed to do before I could be finally connected. According to them, they had still not been paid by the installers. I began phoning the installers almost every day to try to chivvy them along. Once they finally paid up, EDF did their part of the work fairly rapidly.

The next stage was for the installers to send out another electrician to run cable between the transformers in the barn and the meters in the kitchen. Once again I had to keep phoning the installers daily to get an appointment. Every time I was promised that someone would phone me back within forty-eight hours. They never did.

The people on the switchboard were clearly getting as bored with me phoning as I was of calling. I tried to get through to someone in authority, without success. Funnily enough, as soon as I mentioned my discontent on their own Facebook page, a manager phoned me and assured me that I would get a phone call 'before the end of the week' to make an appointment for the electrician. There was no call.

When I got a call early the following week, I assumed it was at last to fix an appointment. Instead another eastern

European voice said he was the electrician and would be with me within ten minutes. I was just on the point of going out. No-one had told me he was coming. I still had the dogs to walk.

I told him to give me twenty minutes and, on arrival, to wait in the van until I told him the dogs were safely fastened up. I didn't want him to get bitten by Ci before he had connected me up.

When Basil, who was from Moldavia, for a change, saw the location of the two things he had to connect up, there was another lot of teeth-sucking and head shaking. He talked about having to run cables up through the roof, across the attic, down through the shower room and bedrooms. I told him just to do the quickest and easiest job possible, as by now I was thoroughly fed up with the whole thing.

Poor Basil told me it was common for sub-contractors like himself to arrive at homes to find no appointment had been made. He travelled from Paris, so it all made complications for him and his schedule when he couldn't access the properties. In the end I settled for a fairly ugly black trunking along the front of the house and the side of the kitchen, just to get the job done.

All that now remained was for EDF to come and give the final all clear to the installation then at last, eight months after the panels were installed, I was able to throw a switch and a little green winking light on the meter board in the kitchen showed me that my panels were finally doing their job.

Of course, I might have guessed the tale of woe wouldn't end there. As I sat down that evening for my usual watching of Coronation Street, my favourite British soap opera, I found I had absolutely no satellite signal whatsoever. When I went out to check, there were clear marks on the satellite dish where Basil's young assistant had leaned his ladders whilst drilling a hole in the wall, knocking the dish completely out of alignment.

It cost me sixty euros to get someone out to tweak the dish

to retrieve the signal. I phoned the installers who told me to send the bill, which I did. I'm still waiting to hear what they are going to do about it.

Chapter Twenty-five
The Lost Boys

The visit of my old and dear friend Alex was going to be the highlight of 2013 for me. We'd known each other for more than thirty years since Alexander Beetle, as I always called him after the A. A. Milne poem, had first come to my riding centre, which was situated on top of a windswept Welsh plateau.

He had paid a short visit to the Pink House when I first moved to France but I dearly wanted him to see my own place. For all the time I had known him, I had nagged him about his smoking and the damage it was doing to his health. He knew it well enough, as his father had died of lung cancer. But smokers always assume they will just go very quickly with a heart attack, or succumb to cancer. What so many don't realise is the long, lingering living death which smoking can inflict.

When I knew Beetle first he was a lithe, fit, healthy-though-smoking hippy, weighing a trim eleven stone, capable of helping me look after more than twenty horses, and sometimes managing the place for me on his own in my absence. Now he was seventeen stone and unable to walk more than ten yards without becoming too breathless to continue. He had finally stopped smoking. A surgeon telling him to stop immediately or risk losing one or both legs had done that, at least. So the first question was going to be, how to get him here?

He'd had a recent bad experience of rail travel in the UK

when the promised disabled assistance had failed to meet him to transfer him between trains, so he was loath to take the risk again, especially to travel abroad. As he loves flying anyway, we decided to use Air France, flying from Birmingham to Paris and then taking the connecting flight to Clermont-Ferrand.

I made numerous phone calls, in French and in English, to make sure every base was covered for disabled assistance. I explained at length this was someone who simply could not walk more than thirty feet, although he would probably manage to get himself very slowly up and down the steps onto the smaller plane on the Clermont-Ferrand hop.

What could possibly go wrong?

The flight was on time into Clermont-Ferrand and I was there ready to greet Beetle. I was pleased to see him being brought into the baggage reclaim area in a wheelchair which was great, it meant Air France had taken on board his needs. I'd brought Mother's old wheelchair to ferry him from there out to the van, so we thanked the man doing the pushing, made the transfer and let the man go.

Baggage safely collected, the dogs, who were in the van, enthusiastically greeted their Uncle Beetle, Fleur for the first time, and it was definitely mutual love at first sight. On the drive back to the grottage, Beetle told me what his actual experience of disabled assistance had been.

There had been no trouble at all at Birmingham, but things had gone awry at Charles de Gaulle Airport, in Paris, which is a very large one. Despite me explaining carefully that the passenger in question had virtually no mobility, poor Beetle had been dumped, without a wheelchair, a very long walk from lavatory or restaurant, for a four-hour stopover.

On arrival at Clermont, the disabled assistance had consisted of the quite small man I had seen with the wheelchair, who arrived empty handed to the plane, and had simply walked backwards down the steps in front of Beetle with his arms outstretched, presumably to break his fall. I'm all for optimism, but had Beetle been unsteady on his feet, which was not the issue, a seventeen-stone six-foot hippy, falling from a higher position, would probably have sent the man plummeting down the steps to land, in the words of the old song: 'on the tarmac like a pound of strawberry jam.'

But Beetle was here, and we were going to have a wonderful three weeks. So he would not be worrying about the return journey throughout his stay, I made a few phone calls to express my disgust in the service to date and was ensured all would run like clockwork on the return trip.

Beetle's experience of France, apart from his brief visit to the Pink House, was based on trying to hitch-hike round it many years ago, where he'd formed an impression that matched the stereotype, of arrogant, foreign-hating Frenchmen. As it was so at odds with my own experiences to date, I was determined to show him the Auvergne as I knew and loved it, kind, friendly people, wonderful food, and stunning wide-open spaces.

Of course, one of the first things to show Beetle was a *vide grenier*, an attic sale, so typical of rural French life, and luckily there was a small one in a little mountain village within two days of his arrival.

I had the tyres of Mother's wheelchair pumped up to a level which had been fine for her, completely forgetting she weighed less than half of what Beetle did. As I started to push him around the sale, it became clear that the tyres were far too soft to get very far, so I stopped and got the bicycle pump out. Within moments, several kind people had stopped to ask if I needed help, and I gladly accepted the offer of one man, who did the job for me.

The next day was another *vide grenier*, in another location. A much bigger one this time, and I knew that the parking was some distance away, downhill from many of the stalls. Because it was so large, the car park was stewarded, so I asked the man on the gate to let us park as near as possible to the road, because of my wheelchair passenger. Ever helpful, he moved tapes to make a special parking space, just for us, and assured me if I had problems pushing Beetle and the chair over the rather rutted field, he would summon up some reinforcements who would, if necessary, lift and carry chair and passenger to the smooth surface of the road. Beetle was starting to get the picture.

The important thing was that all these generous acts were being done spontaneously by kind-hearted people, not by anyone forced into making disabled provision by any kind of law.

I was anxious to share my love of my new home, so wherever a wheelchair could go, we went. When the chair was not possible, I lent Beetle the electric bike. We ate out frequently, and Beetle got to discover wonderfully simple but delicious regional dishes like *truffade*, potatoes and garlic with local cheese, all cooked together in a pot until the cheese melted, *aligot*, with similar ingredients but in a different form, and *pounti*, baked almost like a meat loaf and made from wheat or rye flour, eggs, milk, chard, prunes and bacon or sausage. Then there were the five famous regional cheeses, Cantal, Salers, creamy Saint Nectaire, and the two blues, Fourme d'Ambert and Bleu d'Auvergne.

My new dietary restrictions made it tricky for me, but wherever we ate, someone would make an effort to produce something I could safely eat, even if it was simply a massive bowl of mixed salad, with added extras like artichoke hearts. But try as I might, it was always going to be difficult to explain to the French that I simply could not eat bread, no matter how delicious, home made by them or otherwise.

Another of the biggest points of contention between the French and the British, after the Hundred Years War, is always going to be who did what in the Second World War. 'Cheese eating surrender monkeys' is, sadly, a stereotype idea of the French that some people still cling to. Of course Marshal

Pétain's notorious Vichy government did ally itself with Germany, but there was also the *maquis*, the French resistance, who made a significant impact on the outcome of the war. Some of the bloodiest battles between the *maquis* and the Germans took place in the Massif Central.

Beetle was fascinated by war history. His father had driven a mine-clearing tank on the beaches of Normandy, so he recognised more than most the debt owed to the *maquis*. We put on our list of sites to see some of the *maquis* memorials and museums of the region. One of them, at Estivareilles, meant me venturing a short distance outside my beloved Auvergne into the neighbouring Loire.

The village was the scene of a battle between the resistance and a German armoured column, making their way to Saint-Étienne, to join others marshalling there and heading for Normandy. Although heavily outnumbered, the resistance were victorious, blocking the advance and securing a German surrender. There is now a museum in the village, dedicated to the history of the twentieth century, including a large section on the war. We were thrilled to discover one of the volunteers who ran the museum was the daughter of a *maquisard* with many authentic stories to tell us of those times

I'd arranged to take Beetle down to the Cantal to stay in the same funky yellow chalet where Jill and I had holidayed. I knew he would appreciate the *estives*, being a former dairy herdsman who retained his love of cattle. This time there were quite a few people staying at the site. We had booked an evening meal, to save me from cooking after the journey, and we sat down at a big refectory table with the two owners and a dozen or more French people, from all over the country.

The conversation was fast, non-stop and largely hilarious. As in any group, there was one joker, who had an opinion on everything and had to share it with us all. Alex kept up valiantly with his minimal schoolboy French, and I helped him out when he needed it.

We visited the cattle sale site and stopped for a cold drink at an *auberge* on top of the plateau where we were served by a dreadlocks-sporting hippy, who then promptly fell asleep sprawled on a chair in the dining room. We were joined by his wife/partner/sister/significant other – we never did find out which – who spoke impeccable English and was a delight to talk to. We bartered over a copy of my book, Sell the Pig, which she insisted on paying for and I wanted to give her as a gift as we'd had such a wonderful time. In the end I settled on a huge lump of home-made Saint Nectaire cheese in payment – a good trade.

On the way back from our stay in the Cantal, we had arranged to make a detour to the south east to take in two famous points of interest. The Garabit Viaduct is a stunning four hundred feet high railway arch bridge, built by Gustave Eiffel, which, when it opened, was the highest in the world. Our chosen route took us underneath the bridge for the most spectacular views.

From there we made our way to Mont Mouchet, where French resistance fighters gathered in an attempt to prevent German forces from the south converging with those in Normandy. *Maquis* losses were heavy, with an estimated two hundred and sixty killed and one hundred and eighty wounded, with an additional one hundred hostages executed by the Germans.

The summit of Mont Mouchet culminates at nearly fifteen hundred metres, with a commanding view across the surrounding countryside for miles, an important strategic point. The *maquis* had fought a long, hard and bloody running battle all the way up the road to the summit, trying to hold back the Germans.

At any spot where some of them had fallen, there was a small roadside monument giving their names and ages. I was shocked by how young some of them were, many no more than teenagers, sixteen, at best. We stopped at each to pay our respects. It was intensely moving.

As we neared the summit, we drove through woodland, some of which was old enough to have been there in 1944, at the time of the battle. I kept having the most bizarre sensation of seeing men, young boys really, with rifles, in the woods to the side of us as we drove, but of course, there was no-one there when I looked more closely. Was I seeing the spirits of the Lost Boys, those who never came home? Was it a trick of the light? I never knew, but I certainly saw them.

At the end of the track, there was a large parking area and several monuments. The museum was still closed for lunch so we made our solemn and reflective picnic whilst waiting for it to open. Beetle was determined not to arrive in his wheelchair being pushed by me; he wanted to pay his respects to the Lost Boys and the men who never came home by standing on his feet. So we walked very slowly over to the tall monument, me following behind with the chair in case it was needed, then on down the slope to the museum. I'd lent Beetle my shooting stick to perch on for the frequent stops he needed to make.

The person in charge of the museum was an attractive young girl who barely looked out of her teens but was probably older. I wondered what it was like for her on dark winter's days, alone in a place with such tragic history. I wondered, too, if she had ever seen the Lost Boys, perhaps as she drove back down alone at the end of the day, the last person to leave the mountain after locking up.

The visit made a profound impact on both of us. We had had so much fun, seen so many wonderful things on Beetle's three weeks in the Auvergne. We'd laughed a lot, relaxed, eaten with friends and generally had a brilliant time. But somehow after Mont Mouchet, we were both acutely aware of how much we all owed to those young *maquisards* who gave up their lives in the many running battles around the area.

Small wonder that the French still take the whole business of remembrance much more seriously than the British do. May the eighth, Victory in Europe Day, is a national holiday in France. Each small town, sometimes even each village, has some sort of Remembrance Day parade for the eleventh of November, also a national holiday. I was incredibly touched by the parade in Olliergues, as I stood to attention whilst the Marseillaise was played and the lowered standards were raised, some still carried by Old Boys who had served in various conflicts.

Now when I hear the 'surrender monkeys' comment, I think of those boys in the woods and I have to bite my tongue – very hard indeed.

Chapter Twenty-six
'Elf and Safety'

One of the biggest differences immediately apparent between rural France and the UK is the attitude towards 'Elf and Safety. I'd worked in three further education colleges in England and Wales, lecturing in equine studies to both mainstream and special needs students. I'd also owned a holiday riding centre and managed a large commercial equestrian centre, so I'd undertaken endless training and qualification in risk assessment and management.

Taking students anywhere for any reason in the current safety-mad climate had become a nightmare. Writing risk assessments for a subject involving such dangerous creatures as horses took up considerably more of my time than actually planning or delivering lessons.

When a colleague and I wanted to take a dozen students on a minibus to see the Horse of the Year Show at the National Exhibition Centre in Birmingham, preparing the risk assessment folder took us days. The ultimate piece of lunacy for me came when we were informed that, under college policy, we must include a copy of the Centre's third party insurance certificate in our dossier.

On a scale of one to ten, how likely was it that somewhere like the NEC was not fully insured to admit the public? I had visions of having to phone them up and say: 'If you don't send me a copy of your insurance, we're not bringing our twelve students to your sixteen thousand-seater arena, see how you like that, so there!'

I'm not saying the French take unnecessary risks. They just generally seem to be less paranoid, and also to expect people to take some degree of responsibility for their own safety. It was nothing to go into shops, cafés and the like and find cleaning staff at work, so have to pick a careful way over trailing cables from the vacuum cleaners.

I was once moved to write a tongue in cheek risk assessment to illustrate the difference between my experience in the two countries, which I posted on Facebook. It really does typify the difference, although with a little poetic licence. This is what I wrote:

English Risk Assessment: in store cleaning during customer footfall.

Risks Identified: Trailing cables - trip hazard.

Measures to implement: Place prominent yellow hazard signs at all possible approaches to the hazard by customers, including overhead in case of abseiling from the ceiling. Signs should be in all languages likely to be spoken by customers to the store, including all the principle languages of the EU. An audio version should be available for the visually impaired, as well as signage in Braille. The warning should also appear in pictogram form for unaccompanied children and in comic sans capitals for those with reading difficulties.

French Risk Assessment: in store cleaning during customer footfall.

Risks Identified: None - customers should look where they're going and learn to pick their feet up.

I know, from running horse shows at the equestrian centre I managed, how much paperwork it takes to run even a modest one, and what things have to be in place, including required numbers of first aiders on duty, car park stewards and the like.

For a country which adores fireworks as much as France does, I'm always amazed at how relaxed things seem to be in the rural areas and how little evidence there is of obsessive safety planning for everything.

Every small town in the region has fireworks for things like their *fête patronale*, or parish festival. Bonfire night, of course, does not exist, being an English tradition, and certainly in this area, there are not spontaneous private fireworks displays for anything and everything, going on for days as in the UK. Mercifully, for those of us with dogs like Fleur who are frightened by loud bangs.

Instead the displays are professionally staged and spectacular. The New Year is marked by an exuberant burst of sound and colour, just as midnight chimes. The French National Day, fourteenth of July, is another excuse for pyrotechnic excess. It marks the anniversary of the beginning of the French Revolution with the storming of the Bastille in 1789.

Olliergues is perfectly situated to host spectacular firework events, and the geography of its layout gives it its own safety measures. Built at the bottom of a steep river valley, its ancient château sits high on one bank, overlooking the town. On the opposite bank, steps climb up the steep bank to link the town square to the road above. Townsfolk, and those of us from the outlying villages, flock to the steps for the perfect view of the spectacles, where fireworks are let off in the courtyard in front of the château.

The town also hosts a 'fire festival' which, had I been wearing my risk manager's hat instead of my interested onlooker's hat, would have given me the vapours. The first time I attended, it was without a doubt both the whackiest thing I had ever seen, and the most fun I'd had in ages.

A small crowd assembled on the cobbled market square in

front of the *mairie* to see what would occur. There was a three-piece band, comprising a very good clarinettist, an older man with a pony tail and a tambourine, and a guitarist, playing very good gypsy jazz, which made even creaky old me want to jiggle about to the rhythm.

The town's mayor was there, carrying, in one hand, the sort of weed sprayer used in an average garden, which probably held less than a gallon of water. With him was one of the library ladies, the one who had kindly shown me round on my first visit.

There were two men who were straight off the set of 'Those Magnificent Men in Their Flying Machines'. They wore long leather coats and old pilot helmets with ear flaps, with flying goggles pushed up on top of their helmets. Both had trousers tucked into boots, and wore heavy gardening gloves. They had a small hand cart with them.

When the onlookers were all assembled, the two fire-pilots set off, walking round the town, closely follow by the gypsy jazz trio. Behind them came *Monsieur le Maire* with his hand pump and Library Lady, with her arms outstretched, to stop eager children rushing past her, then the rest of us, in an orderly, though eager, flock.

One of the two men dropped unguarded lighted flares at the side of the narrow paved walkways as we went. They looked a bit like big fire-lighters, and blazed merrily inches away from the ankles of passing children and adults alike. As we arrived at the church, the second man took something out of the handcart and went up the slope to stand in front of the church above us.

The object he now held aloft was a lit Roman candle, which he clasped in his gloved hand, whilst the smouldering sparks rained down on us like a passing shower. The mayor stood poised with his hand pump in case any of us spontaneously combusted.

The spectacle was repeated as we trudged on round the town, between the tall buildings. At each stopping point, the fire-pilot would do something even more bizarre, like balance the lit firework on his head – no wonder he wore a helmet! And all the time the wild gypsy music played, whipping us all up into an excited frenzy which made such dangerous activities seem perfectly normal.

Fortunately for our nerves, the fire-pilot saved his most spectacular trick for near the end of the procession, which took us quite close to the fire station. At least the *pompiers* would not have far to come if the worst came to the worst.

Monsieur le Maire and Library Lady ushered the flock back to all of about three feet away from the action. Fire-pilot produced two brass oil lamps, straight out of Aladdin, filled them up with spirit and set both on fire. Then whilst the gypsy jazz whirled into a dervish frenzy, Fire-pilot spun round and round in demented circles, pouring the blazing liquid in a splashing stream which bounced perilously close to the onlookers.

It was the most insane thing I had ever seen. It broke absolutely every 'elf and safety rule imaginable, and probably some which had not yet been written. It was also one of the most amazing spectacles I'd ever witnessed, and the wild music was ringing in my ears and somehow coursing through my veins even long after it was all over.

It was not the only occasion I was to have wild music ringing in my ears. The bar-restaurant I liked to visit to meet up with friends often had social occasions. *Vide greniers*, arts and crafts, Christmas markets, book signings for me, and all manner of things. When they advertised an Irish night, I was determined to go, since Irish folk music is my absolute favourite. As I hate driving in the dark, I booked into a nearby camp-site to make a night of it, which worked out very well as the following day I was taking the dogs to an *atelier sniff-sniff*, a scent workshop, at our dog club, which was close by.

I arrived in good time at the bar so I could park the van directly opposite to keep an eye on it. Not for a moment that I was worried someone might try to steal it, or even to break into it, but the dogs were, of course, inside, and I was not sure what their reaction would be to the Irish pipes.

In fact the band were already there, starting to tune up, and the piper was playing bagpipes rather than the traditional *uilleann* pipes, or elbow pipes, of Ireland, which are pumped by the elbows rather than blown into.

As almost everything does in France, the evening was going to revolve round a meal. Big refectory tables were laid up, leaving a small space at the end of the room for the band members to install themselves. As I was on my own, I found myself sitting at the head of one table with my back to the band, inches away from the piper.

The band comprised the piper, who also sang lead vocals, a lead guitarist, a bass guitarist, a female singer and a drummer, who was quite new to the ensemble. An Irish band they were not, although they sang a few Irish songs including one of my favourites, The Foggy Dew. They sang a mix of traditional Celtic songs, some French folk songs and bizarrely, some Queen numbers! The woman guitarist played lead guitar for that and was really good. The room erupted into hand- clapping and table-thumping enthusiasm for those pieces.

My ears were ringing from the close proximity of the pipes. It would probably take me some time to hear properly again, but it was such good fun it was well worth it.

The piper was wearing a kilt as is traditional in some parts of France as well as Scotland and Ireland. Inevitably, the subject arose of what is traditionally worn under a kilt. As the piper was speaking, his fellow band members began chanting *'l'éléphant, l'éléphant'*, and he began slowly to fold back his kilt from the hem. This was clearly going to get interesting.

Almost everything is a family occasion in France and this was no exception; there were youngsters present. I was sitting between two young English teenage girls, one a keen budding writer to whom I had been chatting between sets. Her mother attempted to cover their eyes, but only in a jokey way.

Finally the kilt was fully rolled, revealing a blue elephant's head posing pouch, covering whatever, if anything, the piper did wear under his kilt.

Only in France!

Chapter Twenty-seven
Whodunit

Little Olliergues, population less than eight hundred, had a lot more going on than many larger towns I knew back in the UK. Many of the activities centred around the library, even though it was only open three half-days a week.

When I'd first joined, Library Lady had mentioned to me the '*classé polar*', a reading circle for detective novels. It was organised by a group of the libraries in the area. Five crime novels were selected, with a theme. People who signed up had about four months in total to read them, borrowing each for a period of up to two weeks. At the end of the set period, there would be a get- together of all the readers to discuss and evaluate the books and vote for their favourites.

To begin with, although I always read in French, I wasn't confident of my ability to read fast enough to keep up. I was worried about blocking books others were in a hurry to read as I stumbled my way through them.

At the start of my third year in the grottage, when Library Lady once again brought up the subject, I decided to give it a go. I was now the proud owner of a Kobo electronic reading device. Sometimes I even remembered how to use it, though not invariably.

Although enough of a Luddite to prefer a real paper book, I was slowly starting to come to terms with the electronic book age. Particularly since sales of my own books in ebook format were always much greater than those of the paperbacks. Since my hands and wrists were starting to suffer a bit with their arthritic conditions, I did find holding the Kobo in bed at night much better than a real book, especially a thick one. I decided that I would give the challenge a go and would buy at least one of the books for my Kobo, probably the thickest one, so I was under no time pressure to finish it.

We were all duly summoned to the library one Wednesday evening for the opening night, to discover what delights lay in wait for us. About a dozen people turned up, many of whom I already knew by sight, and there were several of the librarians and volunteers from both our library and the main one for the area.

There were only two men present amongst the ladies, one, the inevitable class joker, determined to laugh at everything and make the rest of us laugh with him. The other man was one who asked questions about everything, then questioned the responses to his original questions.

I was now on at least '*bonjour*' terms with most of those present and had even graduated to *la bise*, a kiss, from others, including Library Lady. I tried to imagine what consternation it would cause if English librarians greeted their borrowers with a kiss on both cheeks.

There was one older lady I often saw around town who was always, as the French say, *sur son trente et un*, always dressed up to the nines; loads of make-up, almost theatrical slap, and always sparkly, glittery eye-shadow. She favoured colourful and flowery clothes and always topped off the ensemble with a flamboyant artificial flower in her dyed hair. She lived locally and on colder evenings, would come to the gatherings still wearing her sparkly velvet slippers, for warmth.

One of the librarians introduced the evening and told us the theme this year would be 'serial killer enquiries'. She had two copies of each book and held the relevant one up as she told us a little about them. There were two by French authors, two by

American writers and one by a Greek.

She gave a potted biography of each author, then a brief synopsis of each book. By the time she had got to the third one where the cause of death was decapitation, The Joker asked her if she had not made a mistake and if the actual theme was death by beheading. She assured us they were not all so blood-thirsty, but they were all murder-mysteries.

Next we were handed leaflets about the books and what we had to do, then there was a scramble to grab a book, any book, so we could get started on the challenge. I selected one by Craig Johnson, from the Sheriff Walt Longmire series, which I'd already discovered and enjoyed. They were set in Absaroka County, Wyoming, and Jill and I had visited an area not far from there when we'd done a trail ride in the Washakie Wilderness. Quite a few of his books had been translated into French. Titles are always hardest to translate so 'Another Man's Moccasins' had become *'Enfants de Poussière'*, children of dust, which is what I laid claim to.

I was gutted to discover Craig Johnson had made a visit to the area where I now lived just a few months earlier and had done a talk and book signing in a little village just a few kilometres from my house. Somehow I'd missed the advertisement for it, or I would definitely have gone.

Once most of us had got something to read, it was time for the inevitable spread of food without which no French occasion, not even a library reading circle, was complete. There was wine, of course, but also soft drinks, with bread and *charcuterie*, assorted cooked meats, neither any good to me with my recent diagnosis and preference not to eat dead mammals.

I was getting used to being looked at as if I was an alien species when I said I couldn't eat bread. The locals found it infinitely more bizarre that I was not allowed to eat bread than that I was an eccentric middle-aged Englishwoman living alone in their midst. Bread was such a part of daily French life, people couldn't contemplate living without it. There must, of course, be other coeliacs in the area, but I certainly hadn't met any yet. If Frogification applications were governed by eating bread, I would stand no chance.

Library Lady was most solicitous when I explained I was not allowed to eat bread, not just that I was a fussy eater, and she was determined to find something I could eat. Luckily, there was a bowl of mixed dried fruit and nuts which was likely to be safe, so she kept passing that in my direction.

The libraries in the area also had an excellent initiative to help especially their older members to become familiar with such modern wonders as an electronic *tablette,* that strange new computing device which was as yet totally unknown to me.

When I'd first started out in journalism in the seventies, there were no computers. Some offices I worked in didn't even have the luxury of electric typewriters, they were still on manual ones. In one, I even had to supply my own.

I'd learned to touch-type the old fashioned way, with a tea towel over my hands and the keyboard, bashing along to 'Jimmy Shand and his Band'. It was a great skill, one I'm glad to have learned, and I got up to a really good speed, especially on an electric typewriter.

In the 1980s I'd upgraded to a word processor and thought I was absolutely the bee's knees with that. It wasn't until the change of millennium, when I started out in copywriting, that I really had to get to grips with a computer and things like e-mail.

By now I could use my PC well enough for all my daily work and leisure needs. I'd tried a Mac when Robin, a very kind old friend, sent me one as a gift but couldn't get to grips with it at all. Everyone kept telling me how 'intuitive' they are, but clearly I don't 'intuit' on the same wavelength as Apple, so the MacMonster, as I dubbed it, was soon relegated to Skyping, some word processing and watching DVDs.

Trying out a tablet was going to be a new challenge and one I feared I was not going to find all that easy, based on my performance to date with the Kobo. Because of the carpal tunnel syndrome in my hands, my fingertips were not as sensitive as they used to be. I often found it hard to feel whether I had touched the screen at all, too hard, or not hard enough.

The librarians of the area had gone to great lengths to prepare us a whodunit with all the clues available either online from our homes, or stored on one of the tablets which we could use whilst in the library.

The whodunit revolved around the theft from a library exhibition of a first edition of the magazine Spirou, a popular Franco-Belge comic strip publication. We were given details of the five prime suspects and their interviews with the police investigating the crime. Armed with their answers and our tablets, we had to check out their alibis and find the one whose story didn't add up.

As the challenge was set by librarians and one of the prime suspects was a librarian, I made the obvious deduction that they were most likely to be the guilty party, but set about dutifully checking all the alibis. In fact as I'd picked up a leaflet before the first evening when we all got together, I'd already been able to do some online checking.

We were put together in small teams, each with a librarian or library volunteer to help us with the tablet should we need it. I found myself with a woman I didn't know by sight and with the Man Who Asked Questions.

As I suspected, my hands were not really tactile enough to manage the touch screen very efficiently without a lot of practice, so we let the woman handle our tablet and just tried to find our way round the various applications loaded on it for where the clues lay.

We had a couple of evening sessions and made some progress, but I found the tablet immensely fiddly and frustrating. The comic strip subject matter didn't interest me at all, so having to sit and watch animated comic strips to find the clues I found boring in the extreme. But I was determined to get to grips with the challenge and to arrive at the right answer by following the clues.

I decided I might get on better working by myself, as long as I could manage to work the tablet, so I opted to go on a Wednesday afternoon, hoping that The Man Who Asked questions was not there. I didn't want to appear rude, but I get so frustrated by modern technology, I am better off by myself until I get the hang of it a bit.

Children in France have traditionally never gone to school on Wednesdays. Instead they have longer school days the other four days of the week, although there are currently moves afoot to change this. As a consequence there are often children in the library on a Wednesday afternoon, and this day was no exception.

I was issued with a tablet as I requested and went and installed myself at a small table, where I was soon joined by a girl of perhaps ten. French children have no reserves at all when it comes to talking to adults, strange or otherwise. My young companion immediately started up a long diatribe about which tablets were best, which ones her friends had, which was on her wish list and so on.

Almost all of it passed over my head, as I was still getting to grips with turning the damn thing on and off. More in hope than anticipation, I started prodding at the screen trying to make things open, and forlornly looking for clues as to the validity of the alibis of the prime suspects.

Most of the time I couldn't make head nor tail of it, but I did manage to establish that the fairy tale about the wide-mouthed frog was indeed a fairy tale as regards an alibi. From time to time, when one of the apps I opened had a particularly loud soundtrack, my young friend would reach over patiently and without comment and simply reduce the volume on my tablet for me. She clearly realised I would never manage to accomplish such a menial task on my own, and she was right. The tiny furled wheel that needed to be manipulated was a bit tricky for my hands, and most of the time, I couldn't remember where it was.

I was starting to get grumpy at my lack of success with the gadget and suddenly found myself perfectly happy to frame the imaginary librarian by dismissing all her alibis as false and putting her forward as the culprit, just so that I could declare the case closed. I wondered how many policemen had ever found themselves in that situation?

But eventually I managed to follow all the clues, check all the alibis and establish that my initial hunch had been right. It was indeed the librarian whodunit and I was surprised and pleased to be awarded a book token as a prize for my correct answer.

Chapter Twenty-eight
A letter

Even climate change sceptics had to accept that the winter of 2013 was a very strange one. Weather in the Auvergne is never entirely predictable, but it tends to follow something of a pattern.

December is often sunny and bright, sometimes a little frosty, occasionally warm enough to sit outside. January grumbles and grumps along trying to decide what it's going to do, warm and spring-like one day, cold wind and driving sleet to cut right through you the next. February is often winter at its coldest. Already I'd experienced minus eighteen Celsius and water freezing up at that time of year. March can be quite raw but the snow is usually easing off by then, ready for sunshine in April and flowers bursting into bloom.

There had been a lot of dire mutterings about us facing the worst winter for a hundred years, so when we had an early snow fall, in October, everyone took it as proof. Only it just lasted the night and was gone by the next day.

In mid-November, I arranged to meet my English friend, Linda, in Olliergues and take her to the nearby artisan soap maker I had discovered when Beetle was visiting. He was after a present to take back for the teenage daughter of a friend, and talking to friends of mine with teenage girls, they suggested nice soap would be more than acceptable.

The tourist office were able to tell me there was such a

place just outside Olliergues, so Beetle and I had visited. It was in a big old mill close to the river Dore. As soon as we stepped inside the light and airy gallery with the products on display, our nostrils were tantalised by an incredible array of scents: rose, jasmine, honeysuckle, vanilla, and just about every essential oil imaginable.

There were soaps softened with asses' milk, mares' milk, goats' milk, hemp oil, honey and shea butter. The choice was almost overwhelming, but luckily the lady serving was delighted to help and could produce soap for any type of skin and any skin problem.

Beetle very kindly treated me to some and I picked one with rose and hemp oil, and one with asses' milk and wild oats. As often happens as one gets older, my skin had become much drier and I had a lot of eczema. It cost me a fortune in special moisturising shower gels, creams and potions from the *pharmacie*.

The change to the organic natural soap had made such an incredible difference, I was in danger of becoming addicted to it. With Christmas fast approaching, Linda had a lot of stocking fillers to buy so we had a wonderful time filling up our baskets.

Afterwards we stopped for a coffee at the little bar in Olliergues. Despite the legal smoking ban, Madame the owner was determined she was not going to stand outside her own establishment in the cold and the rain so was defiantly puffing away behind the counter.

As we drank and chatted, we noticed the rain had turned to snowflakes and they were already starting to stick. We decided it would be prudent to drink up our coffee and head home, especially me, as I had to drive up a long and winding road taking me to the grottage a few hundred feet higher up.

By the time I got there, big fat flakes of very convincing snow were falling and already starting to carpet the garden, which was still green with quite lush grass, as was normal for late autumn.

It carried on dumping down for hours. By late evening, when I needed to let the dogs out to relieve themselves before bed, it was already ankle deep and showed no signs of stopping, or of thawing.

What a good job I seldom close the shutters in front of the only door in and out of the grottage, otherwise it would have been impossible for me to get out by the following morning. There was now well over a foot of snow and it was still falling, with no signs of stopping.

Worse, there was no electricity, which also meant no telephone. My brother and I exchanged e-mails daily and I knew he would be concerned if he heard nothing, knowing how bad the snow could be in this area. I decided to attempt to take the dogs out for a walk and at the same time try to send him a text message to let him know that I was all right but without power or telephone.

The grottage was in a bit of a mobile phone black spot, very much affected by the weather. And it was, as they say 'oop north' in the UK, 'awfully black over Bill's mother's'. In fact the sky was pretty black everywhere.

The first flaw in my plan arose when I reached the gates on my driveway. Almost two feet of drifted snow made them impossible to open, so I had to get my big snow shovel out of the van and dig us out.

A snowplough had already made an early pass along the road, skimming off the worst of the snow from the top, so the dogs and I managed to cross over quite easily. But as soon as we started up the steep track opposite which lead into the woods, from where I could almost always manage to get a mobile signal, all three of us were in difficulty.

The snow was up to my knees and very slippery underneath the surface, so I was floundering about and struggling to put one foot in front of the other. Fleur, who was quite small for a collie, was almost sinking out of sight in the drifts. Poor Ci, who was without doubt the hairiest collie I'd ever known and had incredibly hairy feet, like a hobbit, was very quickly covered in tennis-ball sized clumps of snow which clung to him everywhere, making it uncomfortable for him.

I decided to send a quick text message to my brother, as there was a signal, though not a good one, then head back indoors. I also wanted to make a quick call to EDF to find out if the power cut was widespread and was being dealt with.

At that moment, Fleur nearly jumped out of her skin as first one or two, then a positive salvo of loud cracks sounded, just as if we were coming under sustained rifle fire. For a confused moment, I wondered what an earth the hunters were doing out in weather like that, and wished I'd thought to put on the bright fluorescent orange hat I always wore on designated hunting days.

Then I realised what the noise actually was. The snow had come at an extremely unusual time of year for any quantity to fall, which meant that the trees were mostly still in full leaf. The leaves were preventing the trees from simply shrugging off their cold white burden.

As I watched, branches, and in some cases, entire trees, were simply snapping off and falling. I saw one come down right across the phone-line leading to the hamlet. That would explain why we were without power or phone, if it was happening elsewhere too. The quantity affected must have been colossal as just from where I was standing, I saw dozens going down like matchsticks.

Poor Fleur, who was terrified of any loud noises like gunfire, thunder, fireworks, was unable to tell the difference and was shaking like a leaf and pulling hard to be allowed to go back to the safety of the grottage. I thoroughly agreed with her sentiments, so that's what we did.

Luckily Kevin the Kitchen Range had risen to the challenge and was going well so the house was warm, I could cook and brew up, and I had the little solar camping panels for light, charging my mobile phone, and listening to the radio. In fact our power came back on in just five hours. I knew we had got off extremely lightly. Some parts of the region were to stay without power for almost a week, and one EDF worker was killed attempting to deal with a broken power line.

The phone stayed off for two days but even that was quickly restored, great news for me as it meant I could work once I had internet back on. Our road, though by no means a major one, was kept open and passable with care. My neighbour could have gone out to work, she told me, but Olliergues, where she worked, was without power or telephone, so it was impossible to do any work, and anyway the now unheated offices were too cold to work in.

The snow finally stopped falling, although the trees didn't for some time, and it lay for many days, making walking anywhere, especially with the dogs, extremely difficult. Most of the time I played with them in the garden, throwing toys for them to find and fetch.

My neighbour and I would often chat over the fence and now she was off work, we did so more than usual. Fleur and the neighbour's little Jack Russell, Étoile, would race one another up and down on opposite sides of the dividing fence. Ci looked on, clearly unimpressed at such juvenile behaviour. Had he been a human, Ci would probably have been a solitary old queen as he was incredibly prissy for a border collie.

With the roads having been kept reasonably clear, our *factrice*, post lady, had been able to get through most days, although she always seemed quite a nervous driver. She was also extremely nervous of dogs, quite a problem in her profession. Admittedly, Ci would probably have nipped her ankles if I'd let him get near to her, but I always made sure the dogs were behind the high fence when she was due.

On one occasion, as I was outside chatting to my neighbour, the *factrice* came and handed me a letter from the French *Ministère de l'interieur*, the Home Secretary. It must have been about my Frogification.

What were they going to be asking for next? My blood group? My Brownie pet care certificate? Original copies of all my old school reports? That would be guaranteed to deny me acceptance, certainly. Or was it going to be a letter of rejection, telling me that for whatever reason, my application had not been successful?

I tore open the envelope with fumbling fingers and started to read the enclosed letter without bothering to unfold it. 'Within six months blah-blah-blah a letter from your local *préfecture* blah-blah-blah.'

My heart sank into my boots. Rejection. The *préfecture* would contact me to tell me when I could start the application process all over again.

I'd said to my neighbour where the letter was from so, of course, she was all ears wanting to know what it had said. I mumbled something about having to go back to the *préfecture* for my dossier to restart the application and handed her the still folded letter.

'But you're now French!' she exclaimed in surprise, having taken the sensible step of unfolding the letter and beginning to read from the beginning, instead of halfway down, as I had done in my haste. 'The letter from the *préfecture* will tell you when to go and collect your full dossier giving you French nationality and issuing you with a birth certificate in French.'

'I'm French?' I repeated somewhat moronically. 'Are you sure?'

Of course she was sure. Being a native French speaker, she had no problem in reading the letter, which she handed back to me, with a *'félicitations'*, congratulations, which sounded genuine.

I went back into my house to read carefully through every word of the letter. It was starting to sink in. In record time, for French bureaucracy, I had received French nationality. This was now, officially, my country.

I wondered what Mother would have made of me being

Frogified. Had it not been for the long road to bring her to a better quality of life, would I ever have made the decision to leave the UK, for good?

The sun was shining so I celebrated with a cup of tea, weak and fragrant in true French style, rather than British builders' tea, sitting outside the grottage on the raised deck. I looked across to the west, to the line of volcanoes running due south to the Massif du Cantal.

It had been a long and complicated process to come this far but Mother, was it worth it? Yes, it definitely was, and I hopefully had a few more years left to enjoy my beloved Auvergne to the full, as a native.

So now, get on with it, child.

Fin

The End